Mean Moms
Rule

WHY DOING THE HARD STUFF NOW CREATES GOOD KIDS LATER

Denise Schipani

sourcebooks

Published by Sourcebooks, Inc.
P.O. Box 4410, Naperville, Illinois 60567-4410
(630) 961-3900
Fax: (630) 961-2168
www.sourcebooks.com

Schipani, Denise.
  Mean moms rule : why doing the hard stuff now creates good kids later / Denise Schipani.
     p. cm.
Includes bibliographical references and index.
(pbk. : alk. paper) 1. Parenting. 2. Mother and child. 3. Motherhood. I. Title.
HQ755.8.S334 2012
306.874'3--dc23
                         2011048314

Printed and bound in the United States of America.
VP 10 9 8 7 6 5 4 3 2

For my mother, Carol Schipani

Contents

Acknowledgments

This book would not have been possible without my computer, since I can no longer functionally write longhand (not including shopping lists and birthday cards). I wouldn't have been able to even imagine my name on the cover of a book without my circle of fellow writers, so a first, major thanks goes to my Hos (you know your names) who get it, and give it, in a way that makes my working life infinitely smoother and smarter. Thanks to my most amazing agent, Neil Salkind—for a while there, it seemed only he and I truly believed in this book. For Shana Drehs and Deirdre Burgess, my Sourcebooks editors, a million thanks for a million changes and suggestions that made this book approximately four hundred times better than it would have been otherwise. Genius! Thanks to my parents, Frank and Carol Schipani, for, you know, raising me, and to the rest of my fabulously crazy (in the best way) and wonderful (always) family. A special note of gratitude and warm remembrance to Sister John Andre, my sixth-grade English teacher and the first person ever to call me a writer. And finally, my undying love, adoration, and admiration for My Boys: Robert, the best husband, father, and soccer coach on the face of the planet, and Daniel and James, my heart and soul.

Introduction

My name is Denise, and I'm a Mean Mom.

I've chosen a lot of things in my life, such as what college to attend and what to study, the career that suited me best, and the husband to be my partner in life. And I chose to have my children, my two sons who are, as I write this, eight-and-three-quarters and six-and-three-quarters (they tend, like many kids their age, to value precision). Also, I've chosen to be the kind of mother I feel is best, and that kind of mother is mean.

Let me explain and hopefully in the process give you a good idea of what you're going to get from this book: Being a Mean Mom is, in my view, the surest path to creating good kids and ultimately, of course, good adults, good citizens of the world. I say "mean" not because I'm an ice-cream-denying ogre (I am not!), or because I make my kids go work in the coal mine after the third grade (hey, that's illegal; plus, no coal mines in my area!). I define my approach as "mean" because it's not an easy path to take all the time.

It's mean because it often bucks the prevailing parenting trend. It's mean because it often involves the use of the dreaded *no* word (see Chapter Six). And it's mean because overall it entails taking the long view of parenting by often placing more weight on future outcomes than on present-day happiness. It's like the slow burn of a warming campfire, as opposed to the brief flare of a match.

I love my children in the natural, elemental, unspoken way that most mothers do. But just as love alone is not enough to sustain romantic attachment, it's also not enough to raise decent children into independent adults—progeny to be proud of. You need a *plan*. And it's been my plan, from day one, to be the kind of mother who would keep her eyes on the real prize of parenthood, which is to say, the end game. The good kids.

Now, I can almost hear what you're going to say here: *Isn't that what we all want?* Of course it is. But it's been my view that we may be going about it in the wrong way, or in a way that may produce the opposite of what we seek. We say we want our children to be happy, and happy is certainly a terrific thing to want for these children we love so much. But we forget that we can't actually make another person happy. What we can do, however, is give them the tools they need to define what happiness means to them, as well as the tools to achieve it for themselves.

So here's a sampling of what I mean by, well, *mean*. I carved up my philosophy into manifestos, a list of ten principles I try my best to adhere to, which I'll go into more detail with, chapter by chapter. Here they are:

1. **It's not about you. It's about them.** In Chapter One, I'll talk about how many of today's parents, besotted as they are with their new babies, begin to see the kids as extensions

of themselves, and see their children, as they grow, as re-flections of themselves. But parenting is a weird thing: it's probably the most important thing you'll do in your life (presuming you are not William Shakespeare or Martin Luther King Jr. or whoever, someday, finds a cure for cancer) that is *not* about you, at least not in the final analysis.

2. **Hang on to yourself.** Yeah, I know—at first glance, that seems to contradict the "it's not about you" thing. But listen to what I have to say in Chapter Two: If you submerge your pre-kid personality—your goals, hopes, dreams, likes, and dislikes—into parenting, you'll go looking for that self later and find no one's home. Not only that, but if your aim is to raise independent children, you have to model independence yourself. I promise you, it is possible (and in my view preferable!) to raise your children without losing yourself in them. And in the end, they'll thank you for it.

3. **Start as you mean to go on.** In Chapter Three, it's all about creating *your own* set of rules and principles, right from the get-go. Having a new baby is hard, but I caution you to be careful that you're not setting patterns that are hard to break later. Same thing goes for later in parenting: some things you can wing, like what's for dinner or where you'll go on vacation. But if you wing it with discipline and rules—and especially if you change things up out of fear (fear of a tantrum, fear of being called "mean"), you're just

kicking the can down the road. And don't forget—the end of the road is your child, all grown up. Making good decisions *for them* now is a major way to show them how to make smart decisions *for themselves* later.

4. **Don't follow the parenting pack.** Chapter Four helps you forge your path as a parent without succumbing to peer pressure. Parenting's hardly private anymore—we all watch each other, and some of us judge (and are judged) for our choices. The net result of all this out-in-the-open parenting is that you may find yourself doing things that don't really feel right to you. But you do them because they're what everyone else is doing. Following the pack is for junior high (and it isn't such a great idea for that), not for parenting. From you, your kids need clarity, consistency, and the sense that you know what you're doing, although it's perfectly okay if you don't know what you're doing sometimes.

5. **Take (or take back) control.** In Chapter Five I wonder: who's in charge over at your house? Gosh, I hope it's you. It's tough, no doubt, to be the heavy, but if not you, who? It can seem egalitarian and enlightened to let your kids decide they want s'mores for breakfast (and now and then it's just plain fun!), but when they decide important things all the time, you've got the recipe for chaos. Being in control is sometimes being uncool. But in my opinion and experience, the uncool-est parents raise the coolest kids.

6. **Say *no*. Smile. Don't apologize. Repeat as necessary.**
   In Chapter Six, I offer you my favorite mean-mom principle (you're not allowed to have favorite kids, but you can
   have favorite bits of personal philosophy, and this is mine).
   Put simply, an overuse of the word *yes*—and its cousin, the
   "have it all/have it now" attitude—is turning us, the parents, into giant blobs of mush. And it is turning our kids
   into entitled tots who think the world is theirs with zero
   effort required. A few well-placed and well-timed *no*'s—
   those that fit in with your values and your goals—are like
   spinach to kids. Tough to eat at first, but they grow up to
   love it, and are all the stronger for having swallowed it.

7. **Teach them life skills.** I talk in Chapter Seven about some
   pretty old-fashioned stuff. Cooking. Washing cars. Mowing
   lawns. You know, all that stuff you learned to do as a kid but
   that you don't often see kids doing today in our outsource-
   happy world. So do your kids really *need* to know how to
   make a sandwich or clean a toilet? Maybe not on the face of
   it—but I argue that what kids are missing when they don't
   learn life skills is the pride they feel. Your kids have a right
   to feel that pride. I happen to believe that kids who can *do*
   things are smarter, more confident, and ultimately happier.

8. **Slow it down.** In Chapter Eight, I put on the brakes and ask
   you to consider doing the same. It's no newsflash that we live
   in a rush-rush world. Stores stay open later and later, but even

when they're closed, you can find anything you need, anytime you need it, on the trusty Internet. This is the world our kids are living in, and we have to deal with that. But what we should not do is surrender to the belief that this means they have to grow up any faster than they are inclined to. There's value to slowing down the kind of entertainment they consume (whatever happened to age-appropriateness, I ask you?!) or the fashions they wear (a major reason I'm glad I have boys!), or the tech they are treated to. And we have to be pretty careful, as parents, that we're not the ones rushing them.

9. **Fail your child, a little bit, every day.** Chapter Nine's message sounds scary—fail your child?!—but trust me, it's not. Failing at the whole shebang is not what I'm talking about here. Instead, I'm talking about allowing for the small failures—the fall off the swing set, having to cool his heels and wait for you to be free to play Monopoly Jr., the disappointment of not having his best friend follow him to first grade, and so on—because it's in those small failures and disappointments that a child stretches, grows, finds new brain cells, new reserves of nerve and strength and self-reliance. Simply put, I'm asking that you land the helicopter and let your child suffer the slings and arrows of life as they happen. Within reason, of course.

10. **Prepare them for the world, not the world for them.** In Chapter Ten I ask you to consider the end game, the grown

people you hope to raise. It's easy in a world where you can buy baby kneepads for your new crawler to think it perfectly acceptable to argue your child into the "best" kindergarten class or, later, into a better grade. You want to make the world ahead smooth for your child. I turn that on its head here: Wouldn't it be better, in the long run, to make your child smart enough, flexible enough, capable enough, to handle the world with all its inevitable bumps?

The Original Mean Mom

One way I came by my Mean Mom approach was by genetics, and certainly through the way I was raised. Before I had children, I was musing aloud about what sort of parent I might be, and I let slip to a cousin of mine that I figured I'd turn out, more or less, just like my mother. My cousin blurted out—before her internal filter had a chance to stop her—"But Aunt Carol was so *mean!*" What my cousin was likely recalling were memories of my mother yelling up the stairs for us girls to *quiet down and go to sleep! Clean up those toys! And no, you can't have dessert until after dinner.* (My sister, my cousins, and I spent a lot of time together as girls.)

What she left out of that snap judgment of my pronouncement—although I'm sure she didn't actually forget it—was the flip side of my mother's brand of "mean": at my home, there was dinner on the table every night, on schedule; our home was clean and warm and friendly; we always knew what to expect (though we could also expect a swift reaction if we did something unacceptable). And we learned things: We could clean and cook; rake leaves and stack firewood; make bagged lunches and get ourselves to the bus stop in the morning. When my sister and I were old enough, we cleared up after dinner and made coffee for our parents, who rested in the den with the paper and the TV news.

Our house was orderly and my mother ruled firmly, but in my memory, it was also loving. That said, there was not an abundance of "I'll do that for you's." That our parents wished us to be healthy and strong and smart was obvious. That they wished us to be happy? Hmm...Well, yes, I suppose they did want that—though I suspect not in the way today's parents use the word "happy." I imagine if you could go back in time and interview my mom and dad as they drank their after-dinner coffee, on our 1970's pine couch in our dark-paneled den, and ask them, "Do you want your kids to grow up to be happy?", they'd look up, puzzled, and say, "Yes, happy's nice—but what we really want is for our kids to be well prepared to create the kind of good lives on their own that will give them contentment."

And if you asked them, "But don't you want to *make* them happy?" I could just see my mother setting down her coffee cup smartly. "That's not my job," she might say. If lovingly.

You'd never catch my mother, while she was deep in the parenting trenches, uttering the phrase "as long as she's happy..." To the extent I suspect my mother thought about this at all, she figured that happiness was a corollary of what she *really* wanted for us: that we be independent, self-reliant, and pleasant people. That we follow a well-tread path, avoid as best we can common life mistakes, or at least come through them stronger and wiser, and learn to live on our own two feet.

Today's Mean Mom (That Is, You and Me)

Turns out, my prediction that I'd be a lot like my mom was right, or mostly right. As my boys have grown from helpless infants into the proto-tweens they are today, I've stuck as hard as I can to my Mean Mom principles. As a new mother, I protected myself from sinking so far into a glorification of new motherhood and forgetting the woman I was. I chose the methods of baby care and parenting that felt right to me, rather than following whatever was in vogue at the time.

A couple of years ago, struck by how often that approach (a) seemed to go counter to the tide of current parenting styles; (b) mirrored, in an updated-for-the-new-century way, my mother's approach; and (c) seemed, well, *mean*, I started writing about it. My blog, Confessions of a Mean Mommy, gave me an outlet to explain why I refused to, say, stuff a bag with snacks to feed a toddler when we were only out for an hour. It gave me a chance to explore notions like how having high expectations for good behavior in challenging situations (rather than fretting over how I could distract them, or worse, making excuses for them) could actually result in good behavior.

So yes, with the help of my husband (a firm disciplinarian

with a straight-arrow moral code, mixed with the kind of fun-loving, goofball nature that kids gravitate toward), I've tried, for the last eight-and-three-quarter years, to re-tread the path of the Original Mean Mom with a twenty-first-century update.

It's been a little harder for me than I believe it was for my mother, because while in her mom heyday—roughly from the early sixties, when my older sister was born, to the eighties, when my younger brother was still at home and moldable—being a Mean Mom was the default position of society. My mother didn't have to wonder if it was "mean" not to sign us up for Gymboree classes, or not to play on the floor with us all afternoon, or to drag us along on errands without a treat in sight with which to reward us. These weren't options, much less sources of angst or guilt. For me, being a Mean Mom has been more of an uphill climb, more of a push against the prevailing tide.

My Mother, Myself

It's simple to slide mothers into categories pegged to the times in which they happened to become parents. So, it would be easy to say that my mother was the mother that fit her times; she swam with the tide. But there's always more nuance than that. Even for her times, my mom was perhaps "meaner" than most; her mother-love manifested itself as practical, quietly fierce, and not—as I like to call it—*squishy*. She was emotional, but she was tough.

Far from the product of the kind of child-centric, helicoptering parenting style you see these days, my mother—an only child of older, immigrant, working parents—spent a lot of time on her own, well loved and cared for, certainly, but neither coddled nor fussed over. I don't honestly know if I can draw a straight line from my mother's existence as a child to her determination, when she became a mother herself, to raise children who could make a sandwich, run a washing machine, wield a dust cloth, and stand up for themselves. Maybe the line is sketchier, more crooked. Maybe the real story is that she didn't know any other way; never having been coddled, she simply didn't know how to do it, so fostering independence was her form of mother love, the only kind she had access to.

Here's how my mother and I are the same, but different: When I was about as little as my boys are now, and I woke in the middle of the night and called out for my mom, the large majority of the time she would call back with a sleepy, "Just put your head back down and close your eyes." When I hear that call from my sons' rooms these days, I may wait a few seconds longer than some moms, but I get up and go to them. That is, if my husband doesn't beat me to it, and to be honest he most often does. (And often, "Dad!" is the cry we hear in the night, not "Mom!")

And yet there was one time my mom came to me in the night to offer mommy comfort. To be fair, there was probably more than one, but this one stands out in my memory. I don't remember what was wrong, other than I'd woken up and couldn't soothe myself back to sleep. My room was at the end of the hallway, and as she walked toward my door, the hall light back-lit her, in a long nightgown. In my memory, the nightgown's white. (You get the angel reference, yes? It probably wasn't white, but memory is unreliable and stubborn.) She came into my room, sat at the edge of my bed, put a hand on my back, and gently rocked me back and forth.

It was heaven.

But most of the time, my mother didn't love with her hands, or her voice, but with action. I didn't necessarily see this when I was a child, but I see it now that I'm a mother: You can spend every night at your child's bedside, soothing him back to sleep. But if you don't also teach him, eventually, how to soothe himself back to sleep, you're leaving out half the equation.

Another memory: I was in my twenties, living in the city, and I'd taken the commuter train back home for a weekend visit. My mother picked me up at the station. From the platform, I could see her car, and she apparently could see me and watched me walk to the car. As I tossed my overnight bag on the backseat, I could see it: there were tears in her eyes. Little ones, but they were there. "Did I *make* you?" she asked. At the time I understood intellectually what she meant: "You're so beautiful; I'm so proud of you." But I didn't *feel* it until just recently, when I was watching my boys run back and forth in a backyard sprinkler, their sturdy, healthy bodies shining in the sun, and I thought, "Oh, my God, I *made* that," and my heart felt like it would burst.

You see what I mean, don't you? The love that's fierce and visceral—that all parents feel, of course—but in a mom like my mother, and like me, that love is channeled into an equally fierce and visceral need to see them standing up on those strong legs and *going forward*. Growing up. Growing into good people.

My mother—her upbringing, the times, her personality, her ideals—together prop up one leg of the reason I'm a Mean Mom. But let's not forget the times in which *I* came of age, those in-between years in my twenties, already an adult but not yet a parent, watching, listening, and learning. And already, even back then, butting heads with the prevailing parenting style.

By the time I had my first son, I'd had plenty of time to observe other parents, in and outside of my family. I already knew there were a few nonnegotiables. I knew, for example, that going back to work was simply what I had to do, so I'd have to make peace, and fast, with the idea that I'd be trusting someone else to care for my child. I already knew that while a newborn would zap a lot of energy and erase a lot of opportunities for such previously taken-for-granted aspects of my life like sleep, reading, sex, and cocktails (not to mention long brunches and late nights), I couldn't, I wouldn't, let it consign all of those completely into oblivion.

I knew, in short, that I needed to stay me. My name was not going to be Mom, at least not until my child started using it with his own voice. (That's why, when I think of that one labor nurse who kept calling me "mommy," I still grit my teeth, and it's not in memory of the pain or that she wouldn't let me have a sip of my husband's orange juice. I mean, come *on*, did I already have to sacrifice everything for an 8-pound blob who didn't even have the decency to come out easily?)

I quickly saw the problem was that stubbornly remaining myself—with a career, a mind that craved interesting conversation and reading, and a living room that was not redecorated in primary colors—simply was not in vogue when I gave birth. I knew, as the ads say, that having a baby changes everything. But I refused to believe that it had to alter what was most essential about me.

The parenting zeitgeist, though, gave me the message that I was supposed to happily accept the loss of my coffee table (too dangerous) and its replacement with a Little Tikes kitchen; that I was supposed to adore, if ironically, spit-up on my shoes; that I was supposed to love kid music and feel guilty that I wanted to wash my makeup off when I came home from work before attending to my child (who was perfectly happy in his bouncy chair). I was supposed to view two inches of graying roots and/or a messy, unwashed ponytail and baggy sweats as some sort of badge of honor ("I'm a mom! I can't even take a shower!").

Today's version of ideal motherhood is full of a terrific amount of earnestness, a good-student vibe, a feeling that you have to ace the test and be cheerful pulling all-nighters to do so. *You waited so long! You wanted this so much!* All that was true, for me, but that didn't mean I wanted to give in and give up.

I didn't want it because I was loathe to lose myself, but I also already had a glimmer of understanding: if I drowned myself in the pool of my children, I wouldn't be helping them out in the long run either.

My relentlessly practical nature, which mirrors my mom's,

combined with my inborn stubborn streak make me ill-suited to a loosey-goosey parenting style. I *like* schedules and predictability and order. I *like* to be in charge. I *don't* want to be my kids' friends. I'm *not* afraid of them slamming their doors and telling me they hate me. (Okay, I'm still a newbie on that score, and the times my young boys have done the slamming and the hating are more cute than chilling, but they'll get there, I have no doubt.) I get a surge of satisfaction from hearing that my older son is polite, or that my younger son was a good friend to his pre-K classmates. I know there's plenty I can't take credit for, and they do have an awfully good dad. But come to think of it, credit isn't what I'm after. I'm after sending those polite boys, those good friends, those good men, out into the world.

> Credit isn't what I'm after. I'm after sending those polite boys, those good friends, those good men, out into the world.

I won't do it by being perfect. I won't do it by being their pal. I love my boys to the ends of the earth and back, and I'd be quite pleased if they loved me back even a little bit (a little bit of the amount that I love them is, as any mother knows, itself quite a lot). But that's not what I'm looking for from them.

They don't need a perfect mom.

They don't need a slacker mom.

They need a Mean Mom (who loves too much to go soft now).

[1]

Mean Mom Manifesto #1: It's Not about You. It's about Them.

What ever happened to parents being in control of their own homes, of parents being—you'll excuse the terminology, and I'll explain it in a second—sort of benevolent dictators in their homes? When did we stop being, say, Ward and June Cleaver, who could be counted on, in their 1950s TV household, to be *there*, to be in charge, to have answers as often as they had comfort? That's what I mean by benevolent dictators—with the emphasis on benevolent. And when did we become something more like the sweet but befuddled Mike and Frankie Heck of *The Middle*? The latter are good parents, but they're less in control, and also less above the fray of their child-centric household.

Sometime after the social and cultural upheaval of America in the post–World War II years, parenting became less about how to turn kids from babies into adults, and more about both the parents and the kids growing up together.

You and I didn't come to parenting, in most cases, *hoping* our kid might make it out there in the world someday; we came into it *assuming that we could engineer it so that he'd make it out there someday.*

And when you go forth as a parent with that notion—that you can engineer perfection—you make parenting more about yourself than about your children. Sure, it's about them in terms of all you want for them, but the line keeps getting drawn back to you; because you work so hard at this gig, so earnestly, so self-lessly even, their success becomes yours, everything from a dry pair of training underpants to getting into an Ivy League school. It's about you.

Which is not, ultimately, best for your child, who eventually has to live life on his own terms, not yours, and who also has to ultimately take responsibility for his choices, his mistakes, and his victories.

That's why **Mean Mom Manifesto #1** is **It's Not About You. It's About Them.**

Then and Now

Today's moms might...read an article about the latest sleep technique for babies and spend the next two weeks trying it out—and then hopping on an online forum to extol or excoriate it.

Yesterday's moms would...not have time to read articles about sleep. That is, if they could find any to read.

Today's moms might...get a Tweet about a new day camp opening and frantically try to figure out if she can get her deposit back on the old camp and enroll Junior there.

Yesterday's moms would...day camp? Isn't that why we have a backyard and a sprinkler, and those Tupperware ice-pop molds I bought?

Today's moms might...spend hours researching a local gym that has stimulating-enough baby-sitting for her children, or arrange a stroller-walking brigade in her otherwise graveyard-quiet neighborhood.

Yesterday's moms would...follow along with Jack LaLanne on TV, and try not to trip over the kid in the room.

Today's moms might...arrange the kindergarten class's volunteer glue-and-scissor or secret-reader schedule.

Yesterday's moms would...know who the kindergarten teacher is by sight, probably.

Today's moms might...send around an email chain to find out what class all the second-graders would be in for third grade, then plug the information into a spreadsheet.

Yesterday's moms would...spreadsheet? For what, coupons?

Today's moms might...stop at the drive-through for dinner because soccer practice is on one side of town, ballet's on the other, and Mickey D's is in the middle.

> **Yesterday's moms might...**pick up the rare fast food for the kids' dinner when she is going to the neighbors' for a fondue party that might just get crazy.

The Perfection Trap

Every generation of parents loves their children; that's built in. But in the years between my mom's parenting experience and my own, many more clauses have been added to the broadly accepted definition of "loving your child." As I suspect many of you have found, you don't simply have to provide a good, safe home; food and clothes; education and some version of moral instruction. You also have to nurture your child's fragile ego (and begin with the assumption that it *is* fragile); worry about her friendships *when she isn't even able to speak*; wonder if a nighttime crying jag will leave permanent scars; worry about how much or little to expose her to preschool learning experiences; and in general wring your hands over whether your child is *happy*, and what you might be able do (or buy) to make her more so.

The bar for mothers today has gotten almost impossibly high—all the way to, and nothing short of, perfection.

All of us have felt it: that sense that you have to stay on your toes and alert at all times to what you can do to create a smooth path, an ideal, obstacle-free world for your children, a place in which they can grow up happy (nearly) all the time.

But here's the glaring problem that arises when we try—as

many of us do these days with the very best intentions—to fix it so there are no bumps in our children's lives: It's impossible, as perfection tends to be. So you, the mom, end up frazzled and frustrated. That much I'm sure you can appreciate. But another thing happens: All your attempts to create a fuss-free world for your kid make him less able to figure things out for himself. He ends up expecting that you'll always fix things and do things and prepare things for him. In his mind, not only will you catch him if he stumbles, but you'll make it so that *he doesn't stumble to begin with*. He expects you to always make him happy.

But what I've found is that you don't do your children any favors when you prepare the world for them—instead of preparing them for the world (see Chapter Ten). What my mom, and other mothers of her generation, generally did by default—getting kids ready to face the world, a world that was presumed rocky and unpredictable and sometimes cruel—was turned almost totally on its head by the time I procreated. Our generation of moms has taken it as an article of faith that the world into which we bring our babies is both more complicated and more dangerous than that in which we grew up. On top of that, we're often better educated, have more choices for career and whether we will be working moms, and (despite what we think about our shrinking leisure) have more time. Why not

> Our generation of moms has taken it as an article of faith that the world into which we bring our babies is both more complicated and more dangerous than that in which we grew up.

figure out how to fix the world so it's always soft and sweet for our children? If we *can* do it, shouldn't we?

But again, doing it all, reaching for perfect, creating a smooth and easy world, helicoptering for all we are worth, while it looks and can feel as though it's about the children (aren't we doing all this—the childproofing, the kindergarten applications, the school volunteering—for them?), it also encompasses a big dose of what *we* want, what might reflect best on us.

Ironically, when we're trying our hardest to meet the perfection standards we've all set for ourselves as parents, we end up making the whole endeavor more about ourselves than about our children. It's in the way we frame things sometimes. Ever say to your friends or fellow parents, "Oh, I'm *such* a bad mom!" because you missed t-ball sign-up/didn't nab the popular new DS game before it was sold out/semi-ignored your kid's sore throat and sent him to school anyway? What are you looking for when you say that? Validation that you're not, in fact, a bad mother? Someone to say that even if you missed the sports sign-up this once, the kid is already taking swim lessons and playing soccer? It's like we're all saying, "Who, *me*, perfect mom?!" when inside, we're all aching for perfect.

And it's doing our kids no favors. There are risks if we continue focusing on our own ability to parent, on our own choices, on the ways in which our children change us, reflect back on us, and otherwise are attached to us, rather than looking outward, at our children's futures. The risks of today's brand of parenting include giving our kids an overinflated sense of their own importance as well as making ourselves look like buffoons in front of them.

Overinflated sense of importance

What do I mean by overinflated sense of importance, and how does it tie in with the style of parenting that's taken over in the last generation, the style of parental self-absorption? Kids, as you know, are smart. Like, crazy, scary smart. Their senses are finely tuned-in to you, to how you act and what they perceive you represent. If you are preoccupied with how you're turning out as a parent, to the exclusion of how your child is turning out as a person, they are more prone to end up, well, selfish. (Take a look around. See any self-absorbed parents raising self-centered kids in your school, your neighborhood, your PTA? Thought so.)

Why? If you're preoccupied with your own parenting—and further, if your parenting energies are zeroed in on making things easier for your child (providing 24/7 snacks, being sure he never has a "bad" teacher, mediating conflicts with friends, and so on), you leave a void, a space in which you might have put your energies into teaching kids that the world beyond the home you've created for them isn't actually always so smooth. You could be teaching them that there are inevitable disappointments in life. I know, it's ironic, right? Here we collectively are, thinking that our devoted focus on *being the best parent* was the best possible way to raise a generation of the smartest, most creative kids in the history of the world. But in fact, though we certainly *are* raising smart, creative, privileged, and confident (some would say overconfident) children, our relatively self-centered approach of "it's about us, it's about how we're parenting" may actually lead us to raising selfish kids.

Here are some consequences of this trend:

+ **Kids who can't emotionally manage criticism.** Whether it's a teacher meting out discipline, a friend's parent or neighbor redirecting poor behavior, or, down the line, a boss dressing them down, being on the receiving end of criticism is part of life from early on. Sometimes it's fair and warranted; sometimes it's clearly not. That said, if your child has always been at the center, the winner, the best, and if you've always absorbed most of the heat on his behalf, your child may be more likely to crumble in the face of actual adversities, even small or momentary ones.

+ **Kids who don't feel they have any stake in the homes they live in, the things in that home, or even in the emotional life of their families.** If they're the center of the universe, what happens in a house? How many centers of the universe can there be under one roof? (This is a rhetorical question!) So you may, in the extreme, end up with siblings who pay lip service to loving one another, but who don't necessarily have each other's back, because all of them were made into individual stars.

+ **Kids who feel little genuine compulsion to try their best.** If someone else has always done the trying for them, why should they? If someone else absorbs and excuses their failures, why would they need to try harder to avoid failing to begin with?

+ **Kids who don't feel or display nearly enough gratitude for what they have, the enormous gift that every day is.** It's hard to be grateful if everything you want simply appears before you have a chance to ask for it, or if potential painful moments are erased before they have the chance to sting, even a little bit.

Looking like buffoons to our kids

While babies and very young children believe, and rightly, that you'll meet their needs, part of that is a self-centered (but unspoken) assumption that you have no life other than one of service to them. That's how it should be when you have a baby. But if, as our chil-

> As far as I'm concerned, the worst thing our kids can lose is their respect for us.

dren grow up, we skip the part about guiding them out of that belief, if we keep hopping-to whenever our child has any need at all, eventually we'll look pretty foolish to our children. *Geez, can't she leave me alone already?* Oh, don't get me wrong: they'll still love being waited on, who doesn't? But that doesn't mean they won't see, dimly at first but over time much more clearly, that we're being chumps. It's not easy to respect a chump, an easy mark.

As far as I'm concerned, the worst thing our kids can lose is their respect for us. Because it can lead to:

+ **Kids who expand their lack of respect for you to a lack of respect for their grandparents, aunts and uncles, neighbors, and teachers.** This one truly makes me cringe. I've seen kids laugh at what their grandmother is wearing, or rib their grandfather for his old-man car or taste in music. I had genuinely adoring and indulgent grandparents—they weren't aloof and hardly stood on ceremony—but I *cannot even conceive* of saying anything disrespectful to them. Or not thanking them for a gift. Or...you get my drift.

+ **Kids who, after long practice of having little to no respect for you, end up having little respect for themselves.** You may think that's a leap too far, but bear with me. When a parent spends way too much time and mental energy wondering—aloud, the worst way to do it around kids—if what they are doing is right or wrong or good or bad, the kids start to see their parents as kind of wishy-washy, not very stand-up. What you have there is a total lack of good example, of the kind of quiet, sure-footed modeling that creates kids who do respect themselves, trust their emotions, and feel secure in their own minds, hearts, and homes. *If they have no immediate example of self-respect, how are they ever going to gain it for themselves?*

Don't Forget the Future

All parents can probably use a gentle reminder that their lives won't, and shouldn't, always be lived on the knife's edge of nap-or-not, or how-long-was-that-nap; that they won't always be playing the "what color was her poop today?" game. Babies do get older, and in the process become easier in some ways (harder in others, though). All parents can stand to wave away the fog for a few minutes and remember that the essential they-ness of themselves is still in there, somewhere. That they still have books they'd like to read and movies they'd like to see, yes; but also that they have other uses for their hearts, minds, and brains than whether baby Jane is getting enough sleep.

Stay with it! It's a hard struggle, working out where you end and your child begins. You may think, *But aren't I sup-posed to blur those lines? Aren't I supposed to put the child in the center, with me in the minor, backstage role?* The child is Rocky;

> All parents can probably use a gentle reminder that their lives won't, and shouldn't, always be lived on the knife's edge of nap-or-not, or how-long-was-that-nap; that they won't always be playing the "what color was her poop today?" game.

you're his trainer Mickey. Not exactly. You quite naturally support your child. But you are *not* the sum of your children.

No, I am not arguing that you should take a toddler who just learned to operate the toilet or navigate a spoonful of oatmeal more or less to the general vicinity of her mouth, and shove her out of the nest ("Write when you get work, honey!"). But I am arguing that turning her success with the potty or the big-girl cup into *your* success is the wrong way to go about it.

It's harder, yes, and, okay, meaner to do it my way. But it makes better kids.

They're not ours forever

Now, I can completely understand the impulse to look at parenting as an extension of who and what we are. In a way, it is. When we have children biologically, they are created from us, are attached to and then physically emerge from us (well, us mothers, anyway!). When we adopt children, the process of finding a child and fighting mountains of paperwork and bewildering bureaucracies, or coping with the intense heartbreak of, to use just one example, a birthmother who changes her mind, can be so battering emotionally that we feel, when we've finally made those children our own, exactly the same way. Put more simply, we all bear the scars and endure the pain of having children.

So why *wouldn't* we want to make those children reflect what's absolutely best about us? It seems so right, and yet I argue that it really is all wrong. Not only for us, but for them. If you compress parenthood down to a blip (which it can feel like, right?), what you have to do is get them out of your body and out into the world.

Ever watch nature documentaries? As a kid, I watched *Mutual of Omaha's Wild Kingdom* every Sunday night. These days, kids can glue themselves to Animal Planet, and there's no shortage of public-television shows about animals. What has always fascinated me is how many mothers in the wild—let's take a giraffe as an example since I happen to love giraffes—drop their offspring to the ground when they give birth, literally: a female giraffe doesn't recline to give birth, so her newborn has a ways to fall. Then the mama's version of tough love begins: nudge that shaky-legged baby to her feet. Her focus, the animal-mama's focus, is on getting the baby out, up on his feet, and hopefully not eaten by anything bigger or faster before it has a chance to learn to fend for itself.

For quite obvious evolutionary and biological reasons, we can't nudge a newborn to her feet, give her a rough lick or two to get the birth gook off her, and then passively chew on the highest tree on the savannah while she searches for a teat to drink from. Our big-headed babies have to be born before they're really "cooked," which leads to a prolonged (in the mammalian sense) childhood.

My contention is that we prolong it too far, in our own heads. We could all use just a touch more of the animal version of tough love. Remember, when it's tough (or, well, mean), it's still love.

Shift Your Focus

To my mind, a major means we have at our disposal to help us take the focus *off* ourselves (our parenting, how "well" we're doing, how we look to others) is practicing a little benign neglect, à la those mothers-in-the-wild. Here's what I mean:

+ **Presume your child's competence (rather than assuming her fragility).** If we believe our kids are immensely fragile, even after babyhood, we're elevating our own importance to an unsupportable degree. *She can't possibly get by without me!* Is that really always true? When my older son started preschool, at just shy of three years old, I got an excellent object lesson in this principle. He was taking a mini-bus for the first time. It was all kinds of safe—the bus had car seats and a matron to look out for the little charges. But on the first day, I dutifully climbed aboard the bus with my son to be sure he was okay. No one said anything, but the next day I was informed—gently but firmly—that insurance rules prohibited parents from being on the bus. That made sense logically, and I just as dutifully stepped back thereafter.

  But looking back now, I see the object lesson: I could walk my child all the way to the bottom of the driveway, but after that, he was *fine* getting on the bus without me. Otherwise, what would I have done? Ridden with him to school? Sat in a teeny-tiny chair next to him? Held his crayons for him? You have to assume (within reason) that, as they say, the kids are all right.

+ **Make the big decisions, but don't sweat the small ones.** Decide—based on your research, based on what feels natural and comfortable to you, based on trial and error—what Capital Letter Parenting stuff you'll do or not do: Breastfeeding. Sleeping arrangements. Preschooling, homeschooling, organic foods, you get the idea. But the small stuff? Exactly *what* preschool, say? Or whether your decisions match the prevailing wisdom of the playgroup (for more on this, see Chapter Four)? That's all small-scale stuff that, if you fret over it, makes you and your needs front and center, less so your child's.

+ **Hands off your kids' friendships.** Within reason, of course, you should listen to your kids' musings and tales and shifting-alliance stories of friendships without butting in, much as you might want to. That's his area. I see a lot—too much, actually—of parents who practically keep spreadsheets of their kids' friends. That's her dance-school friend; this is her old preschool crowd; I like that kid and I don't like this one, and so on. Too much of that, and you end up making your child's social life an extension of your own.

+ **Edit yourself from the picture.** No, not the photographs; if you're anything like me, there's a distinct *lack* of pictures of you, post-motherhood, in the family albums! I mean, edit yourself from the picture that is your child's everyday life. Know exactly what's going on in your own home, but *not* everything that's going on at school, or at dance class, or at Cub Scouts, or in your child's junk drawer in his nightstand (I've taken a cursory glance at my son's, and honestly, I have no idea what's going in there!). Be the mom who goes to open school night and doesn't rearrange the books and pencils in your child's desk, because that's his space.

+ **Expect the respect due you as the adult (i.e., you're not their friend).** You're going to find, as you read this book, several mentions of not being "friends" with your kids. Let me get right in here at Chapter One and explain what I mean: Not being friends with your kids is *not* the same thing as being aloof from them, like really old-school family situations where kids sat at the dining room table with their mouths zipped tight, except to say "yes, sir" and "yes, ma'am" to their parents. That's anachronistic and wrong. In my view, not being friends is more about *remaining the parent in charge*, even if that parent is almost slobberingly loving. When parents try too hard to be friends with their kids, they may confuse it with getting down to the level of their kids—emotionally and mentally. Digging into their dramas, adding *to* the dramas, becoming a part of their world in an unhealthy way. Unhealthy because it puts you too far into the picture of your kids' lives, *and* because it leaves a vacancy at the top, at the spot where someone—the parent!—needs to be in control. Your kids actually don't need more friends; they do need parents. They need not just the bodies in the house, the playmates, the snack-dispensers—they need *someone to respect*. Treat your kids respectfully, of course; but expect a different kind of respect in return. The kind of respect that makes it clear: you're the parent, they're the kids.

So that's it: they're the children, you're the parent, and raising them isn't about you, but about their futures. Get that down first, and you're well on your way to mean momhood. Come on over—the view is excellent from here!

[2]

Mean Mom Manifesto #2:
Hang On to Yourself.
You May Need That Person Later
(and So May Your Kids).

Hello, life. Meet baby. *But wait! Don't go away!*

Despite initial panic that I wouldn't be able to get pregnant at thirty-five, I actually conceived our first son fairly quickly. I was also blessed with a trouble-free pregnancy. The only issues I had fitting my pregnancy into my life were the usual: giving up wine, and not being able to wear shoes with buckles or laces in the last four weeks or so. If YouTube had existed at the time, and had I been able to film myself, the morning I spent ten whole minutes trying, and ultimately failing, to strap on my favorite low-heeled sandals would have made quite the hilarious viral clip. I kept thinking, "There has to be *some* way," as though my body were a giant, recalcitrant Rubik's cube I could twist to my will.

Birth, however, was another story altogether. Turns out that birthing babies? Yeah, not so good at that part. I spent two days in (and out, and then back in) the hospital trying to get my firstborn from the inside to the outside. I thought, no question, that he was obviously the most startlingly beautiful, perfect baby ever to have been created (it helped that he had the classic C-section head—no birth-canal cone head). I was more than preoccupied with the usual first-baby stuff, primarily getting him to nurse and wiping that weird black meconium off his impossibly perfect butt.

However. My lovely child was born at 8:00 on a Wednesday morning. And Wednesday was *The West Wing* day, and the *Wing* was by far my husband's and my can't-miss show. By late that afternoon, the doctors and nurses were praising my body's strength; I may have looked like a sack of half-drowned kittens (with a nice case of hormone-triggered acne), but even after two days of labor followed by surgery, I was sitting up in a chair within a few hours. Right after they got me into that chair, all propped with pillows, and after my husband and I had marveled for the seven hundredth time that our perfect son was swaddled and sleeping, we realized: It's Wednesday. *The West Wing* is on. I grabbed the remote but, inexplicably, I couldn't seem to find the right channel on the TV I was probably going to pay too much for. *What was going on? How could this major metropolitan hospital not have NBC?!*

In a panic (we really, *really* loved this show, and no, I will not apologize or even admit it was silly. It wasn't silly; it was *The West Wing*, for crying out loud), I had my husband call a friend who would promise to tape the show for us.

It was *that* important, and the fact that we had it covered was *that* satisfying.

Were we crazy? Maybe. Smug? Possibly. But reflecting back on it now, I believe this story serves at least a symbolic point. Even from the very beginning of my motherhood adventure, I was determined to hang tight to who I was, to not allow myself to morph into someone else entirely, someone I would no longer recognize. Of course I changed; that's inevitable. And although it took a while, I did embrace most of those changes, but I prefer to call them improvements. Like adding an extension onto a house: You can raise the roof, attach a new two-car garage, build a cathedral-ceilinged great room off the back. But if you scan through the home with a practiced eye, you can still trace the outlines of the original structure.

That was me: the old house, with a baby (and all his attendant needs, his accoutrements, and—of course—my outsize hopes and dreams for him) tacked on.

Was this my first act as a Mean Mom? It's not as though I ignored my newborn for the sake of a TV show. For one thing, first-day newborns are, blessedly, sleepy enough that you can actually rest a bit. (It's when you arrive home, usually, that the little guy or girl wakes up to the indignity of being outside the womb— Hey! What's with all this light? And the noise? And where's the food?!—occurs to them and they start crying...a lot.) For another thing, *of course* had my new son needed me at the moment I was fussing about *The West Wing*, I'd have reached for him instantly.

But I do feel this small act of "I'm still me" is what first helped me eventually define **Mean Mom Manifesto #2: Hang On to Yourself!**

The Life-Baby Collision

It's all well and good to say that you want to retain the core of your original self, to claim your pre-mom footprint. It's another to actually do it. The collision of Life with Baby is huge and disrupting, to say the least, but it seems to me that an awful lot of parents dissolve too much of the Life part when they crash into the Baby part. Why not instead brace yourself for the onslaught, so you're prepared (as much as you can be!) to take the baby into your life without allowing the baby to bring your life down around your ears?

Part of what I think happened is that we all started, in the last generation or two, to parent right out in the open, making it easy for all of us to scrutinize one another, as well as measure ourselves against each other. Whereas my mother could wear makeup or not; sign us up for extracurricular activities or not; feed us wonderful meals or boxed frozen dinners; yell at us when she got angry or tired or frustrated, or hug us for being the best kids ever; tell us to go play so she could do her own thing indoors or not; and who would know?

No one. And if no one knew, no one could judge. And if no one was judging, then she didn't have to play up a big act of being Super Mama, or of being *happy* about twisting her life into some pretzel-shaped notion of what a good mother was.

Plus, if *she* didn't know what Mrs. So-and-So or Mrs. What's Her Face next door was doing—or whether her most proximal fellow-mothers were moaning about stretch marks or wondering why they couldn't get the kids to listen or feeling guilty/not guilty for not doing "floor time" with them—she couldn't judge.

The point is, even when modern parents like us let our parenting dirty laundry hang out, we don't actually allow it to *be* dirty. Those sheets are crisp and white and *perfect*. We love it, all of it. We do things like change our email address from Karen.Jones@internet.org to Mom2TwoAndLovinIt@internet.org. Which mom lost track of the original blueprint to the house that was *herself*? And which feels the need to lose herself in the new addition?

Sometimes it's not even a need to lose yourself, but a pressure. What if the working mom declares that she sometimes finds it a relief to head to the office on Monday morning? That may be true of many a working mother, but only the very bravest will admit it. Just the other day, a friend told me about how, after picking up her son from a playdate at the home of a new acquaintance, and learning that the boys played so well that this other mother had hardly noticed they were there, she said, "Well, that must have been a relief to you!" My friend reported that she'd said this because had the tables been turned, she herself would certainly have found it a relief. Maybe she'd have read the paper or watched a few minutes of HGTV. But the other mom looked at her like she had three heads, none of which had "Great mom!" stamped on it. A *relief*? To not have to pay attention to our *precious children*?!

A couple of years ago, an acquaintance of mine asked me if I knew where one of our mutual neighbors—a woman with three kids, two in school and a small boy, and no outside-the-home job—was *going* with that little boy in the mornings. "Oh, I think she takes him to a preschool day-care thingy," I replied.

The acquaintance got her feathers in such a "how dare she send her baby off to day care when she doesn't have to" bunch, I felt compelled to reply, more harshly than I intended, truly, "Not every mother can spend every minute with her kids, you know."

You're supposed to look like you love it. Because someone might be watching, and judging.

Why Do We Care What Other Moms Think?

I doubt it will come as breaking news to you that we moms can be each other's, and our own, worst enemy. Yeah, we can be pretty judgmental. It's my contention that a good chunk of that judgment comes from two places, both related to the notion of hanging on to yourself (or not hanging on to yourself!).

When we watch each other parent, when parenting becomes, as it has, a *topic*, the inevitable result is judgment—of others, but also of ourselves. Maybe we find ourselves wanting, or not measuring up, when we, for example, admit that on the first day of our child's life, we were preoccupied with watching *The West Wing*. Or admit that while we breastfed our newborn son, we were not reading *How to Breastfeed* articles in parenting magazines (or our dog-eared copies of *What to Expect*) but were determinedly (and possibly dementedly) reading *The New Yorker* in an effort to keep up and stay ourselves.

But why do we care so much what others' judgments are? Why should my neighbor care whether another neighbor doesn't work but also doesn't have her toddler home with her all day? Why, when we are working mothers, do we have to keep bottled up not just that we love our work, but that—gulp!—we love being away from our kids? That we like being able to go to the ladies' room solo, say, or shut the office door and eat a sandwich in peace? And why, when we are stay-at-home moms, do we have to present a perfect front, telling anyone who'll listen that we *love* spending the bulk of our days with sticky-fingered folks who don't have all that expansive a vocabulary?

If another mother admits that she's out of her mind with boredom, home with three kids under five, she presents a potential threat to the mother beside her in playgroup who'd rather not confront those feelings. And the working mom can't possibly admit she's either happy how things are, or not so happy and instead insanely jealous of the mom who, from the working mother's perspective, gets to wear much more comfortable shoes and not miss her toddler's discovery of a new worm in the garden.

> And if you're not true to yourself, and if you're not honest, it's hard to be the kind of parent who can keep her eyes on the prize of raising confident, independent people.

There are no true or right answers here, but one of the problems with not hanging on to yourself is not being true to yourself, either. And if you're not true to yourself, and if you're not honest, it's hard to be the kind of parent who can keep her eyes on the prize of raising confident, independent people.

Holding On to Yourself = Raising Good Kids

So, if you are, as I was, careful to preserve yourself as a woman even as you evolve as a mother, how does that help your child? When you are focused on which other mother is doing it wrong, or who is on your "side" in the "mommy wars," you're back to making parenting about you and your choices in life, and not about your kids. Some of the very best things your children can see about you are that:

+ **You are your own person.** It may feel as though if you consciously try to *add* your baby to your life (keeping hold of aspects of the "life" part that feel most self-defining to you) that you're dividing your attention to the detriment of your baby, but trust me, it's the opposite. Instead, when you consciously keep up with whatever it is that floats your boat, from the *New Yorker* to *Dancing with the Stars*, from your yoga class to your gel manicure, you're keeping both: yourself as a woman, yourself as a mother, and expanding both to fill your new life.

+ **You have your own thoughts.** Okay, I know that even the most deeply involved and child-centered mother is not a Stepford automaton with *no* thoughts of her own. But plenty of smart, well-meaning women, believing that to be a good mother they have to be 100 percent into mothering, don't indulge or explore or follow their own thoughts, their own opinions. "Oh, I never read the paper," you'll hear. It's *good* for your children to hear you—even before they understand what you're saying—discussing ideas and interests that have nothing to do with anything related to, well, *them*.

+ **You are honest**. So, fair enough, you can't prop a six-month-old up on the other end of the couch from you and tell her honestly that you feel conflicted about your life as a mother. But you can be age-appropriately honest with your children as they grow about the challenges of raising them, as well as the joys. Part of that will help you remain honest with yourself and in touch with your own feelings, and part of it—a big part—helps your child continue to see you as a real person, not an always-in-service being devoted solely to him.

+ **You are not perfect.** There's a children's musician/singer, Laurie Berkner, who my kids used to listen to. She had this one song, "I'm Not Perfect," which I used to find myself singing all the time: "I'm not perfect/But I've got what I've got." I feel it's a good, humble, straightforward message not only to teach your children, but also to model for them. *I do the best I can, kid—but behind this gal you believe has all the answers, and all the frozen waffles you can possibly eat, is a woman who doesn't always know the answers,* *and also sometimes doesn't make it to the store so, sorry, no waffles today.*

Relinquishing Yourself: It Feels Right, but It's All Wrong

Let's have a look at some things that conspire to make you believe you should dissolve your old self once there's a new baby in your life, the things that feel as though they should be *so right* and *so normal*, but which wear us down as mothers. These are dangerous myths, because they're pervasive and insidious and very much like "wolf in sheep's clothing." We've all seen them, and many of us have probably suspected at some point they were bad ideas, but few of us feel all that free to admit it.

Myth 1: We believe parenting is a test we can ace

That we're more likely to have deliberately created our children compels us to put a capital P on Parenting. In the years since family planning turned parenthood into more of a choice than an inevitability, parenting gradually shifted, almost without people necessarily noticing it, into something that felt more precious because it was more deliberate.

> Before our babies even arrive, we've anticipated ourselves into a corner, planned ourselves into oblivion. And when you invest that much, you damn well better get it right.

With my firstborn, I fussed with the temperature charts and scheduled the sex and read the books. The minute I saw the plus sign on the first test strip, I began investing all sorts of thoughts and feelings and ideas on my child. Now, I'm not saying my parents didn't have *plans* for us—of course they did—but those plans started with something as simple as "let's figure out how to feed her/not drop her/teach her to sleep" and ended there too.

Whereas mothers like my mom from previous generations reacted rather than anticipated, our generation anticipates. A lot. Before our babies even arrive, we've anticipated ourselves into a corner, planned ourselves into oblivion. And when you invest that much, *you damn well better get it right.* And somehow, "getting it right" turned into "giving yourself over to it." Our parenting efforts are a giant, multiple-choice test, and we have to get it right.

Myth-to-reality

Try to quit thinking of parenting as a test, and try to view it as a journey instead. The only "grade" that really matters is that our kids grow up, and it won't matter in the final analysis if, for example, you breastfed for six months or a full year, or if you had to squeeze two kids into a tiny room, or you chose a preschool because your friend's kid went there and you could carpool, even though the one across town was "better."

Myth 2:
We pursue the holy grail of ideal bonding

As modern, "connected" parents, we've absorbed the lesson that we have to bond, seamlessly and more or less instantly, or our child will suffer. As a parenting writer, I've researched and written a number of stories about bonding, and I'm always told the same thing by the experts: Bonding is not an identifiable or "aha!" moment. There's no instant click, accompanied by the swelling of violins as the background fades into pastels and, I don't know, unicorns. It is, instead, a process that is sometimes quick but is just as often lengthy—and occasionally thorny. But sober facts about bonding's true, gradual nature—even if we've heard or read them and grasped them intellectually—don't always register. Some of us still seem to believe that bonding is a moment you can miss if you're not careful, as though it was the president zooming by in a motorcade or your favorite actor walking into a restaurant, and if you stoop to tie your shoe or fumble for your camera for too long, you're out of luck forever because when is Matt Damon coming to your local Panera again? Never.

We, as a generation, have been too careful (think: *good student*) and are too hell-bent on doing everything right to mess with anything as crucial as bonding, so we refuse to see it as a mystery. You read those articles and passages in books and say, "Yeah, yeah, it doesn't have to happen instantly. But it will for *me*." So it should hardly be a surprise that we still end up feeling inadequate if our experience doesn't play out with rainbows and unicorns. One of the reasons is that even as the articles and talking heads on TV tell you it's perfectly okay if you don't have the baby plopped on your chest right after birth, they also tell you—subtly and not so subtly—that there are still things you can (and therefore *should*) do to "fix" the "problem," preferably as quickly as you can.

Here's an example: The story you might have read (and that I, uh, might have written) might say, "If your baby has to be in a NICU for a while, or if you had a C-section and can't hold your baby instantly, you'll still bond, don't worry." But it then goes on to say—helpfully, but also with a fair bit of superior finger-wagging—that you should "be sure you get plenty of skin-to-skin contact as soon as you can" or "make sure you take shifts in the NICU so you can be in reach of your child." There's an awful lot of *make sure you...*, which tends to leave the impression that while it's okay if you don't, it's still better—vastly better—if you do. The subtext: *You're not a bad mother if you don't fall crazy in love within minutes...but you're certainly a better mother if you do.*

Myth-to-reality

Does it go without saying that I didn't bond immediately? I loved my baby, for sure, and I was quite competent at caring for him, but a lot of it felt rote and left me feeling remote. Of course, a lot had to do with the kind of exhaustion that scrambles brain cells like so many eggs. I felt broken and messed up; there were no rainbows. At my six-week checkup, my doctor must have seen (even as her nurse was cooing over my fat, healthy boy) the dull look of fear and pain in my eyes. Gently, she put her hand on my knee and said, "It gets better, I promise. He'll smile soon, and you won't look back."

He did smile, and it did get better—but I always look back. Why? So I could get to this very day and write these very words: If you have a baby, don't expect instant bonding; it's a bad trap. And if that was your past experience, ditch the guilt over it, if you still have any. You love your child; that's all you (or your kid) ever needs to know, and certainly not that you skipped one of those late-night hospital feedings and told the nurse to take him back to the nursery for a few hours. And he certainly doesn't need to know there were times you wished you could pop his squalling newborn self out onto the fire escape. (Who, me? I'm not saying anything...)

Myth 3:
We believe early motherhood
can, or should, be blissful

We feel inadequate when our postpartum lives are messy rather than a bundle of newborn-baby bliss. Who was it that started up this myth that early motherhood spools out in a gauzy, Vaseline-on-the-lens sort of way, as though we're running through fields of sunflowers with our impossibly angelic babies? I'd like to find that person and give her a piece of my mind. But of course it's not a *person*. Myths never start with a person. What happens is there *are* truly wonderful moments (I had them too, really!) and those moments—the ones where your baby is blissed out, drunk on your milk, and giving off that heady newborn scent that gives you the kind of contact high

I'm convinced perpetuates the species—are the ones we repeat to each other. Meanwhile, we hide the uglier truths.

Oh, sure, we share hilarious anecdotes about diaper blowouts and projectile vomit. We grin ruefully over the piles of soiled onesies and the crusty bowls of uneaten cereal left around the house and how we often don't wash our own faces until 3:00 p.m., if then. But we don't talk about how that makes us *feel*, not with real honesty, not at the same level as the way we talk about the bliss.

We don't talk about how the fourth hour of crying slices through our competence and makes us feel like we'll never get a handle on this parenting thing, or how no matter what the books or magazines say, we can't just "sleep when the baby sleeps!" and ignore the crusty cereal bowls. Because the truth is, far from being Hallmark-worthy in feel and sentiment, the early newborn period happens with thuds and crashes, not graceful ballet leaps. That your baby is beautiful is more abstract than all-consuming, because your days—if they're anything like mine were—are a jumble of tears and mixed emotions and a *lot* of messiness. That's leaving out the way we *still* don't talk adequately about issues far more serious than how crusty cereal bowls make you nuts, about the crushing feeling of inadequacy, about the postpartum blues, about depression.

Myth-to-reality

I'm going to say this loud, so read it that way: **If you didn't get the blissed-out end of the new-mom stick, it's not your fault.** You are *not* the only mom in the history of the world who picked up the beautiful "welcome baby!" card someone sent you and didn't get the sweet sentiment written there because it was so far from your own mucky reality. Which doesn't mean that sometimes the reality isn't sweet and perfect, but when it's not? You shouldn't hide it under the couch with the cereal bowls: you should *own* it. Be honest. Tell a new mother that sometimes it sucks—and mean it. Pay it forward

Myth 4:
We believe "mom" and "saint" are synonyms

Earlier in this chapter, I talked about how, in the last generation or two, we've begun to parent out in the open. All thoughts, all feelings are ripe for revelation. But there's a catch: The feelings revealed have to show—prove, really—that you are Saint Mommy, that all you think about is your child. And if you think about something other than motherhood, such as sex, your marriage, or your career, you at least have the decency to be consumed with guilt about worrying over these "side" issues. You have to show, over and over again, that your child has transformed you into something *so much better* than you were before.

Take this Facebook status. If you've seen something like this on one of your friends' walls, you are meant to copy and paste it onto your own (subtext: if you don't, then you aren't as crazy-go-nuts in love with your child and your life as a mother, as those who do repost, with bonus points for figuring out how to make heart emoticons). It went like this, though I'm sure there are other similarly worded examples:

"Mothers' Day Declaration ~ I wanted you before you were born. I loved you when you were born. I saw your face, and I knew I was in love. Before you were an hour old, I knew I would die for you. To this day, I still will. This is the miracle of life. ~ Put this on your status if you have children you love more than life itself."

Of course, I have no problem with you loving your child beyond all reason, beyond anyone's ability to explain it, or much less put it into words. That's the mystery of being a parent, and it happens whether you got pregnant accidentally or planned it carefully, whether you suffered infertility or adopted.

What I do have a problem with is when *other people* try to tell me (not just me, but anyone else) that I'm supposed to feel a certain way about my children and my role as a mother. Especially when that "certain way" simplifies something magnificent into something smarmy and, ultimately, false.

A similar Facebook "declaration" took its triumphal tour through the social network at around the same time, this one asking moms to copy this bit of ick to their status:

"I traded eyeliner for dark circles, salon haircuts for pony-tails, designer jeans for sweatpants, long hot baths for lucky if I get a shower, late nights for early morning cartoons, designer purses for diaper bags, and I wouldn't change a thing!! ♥♥♥ Repost this if you don't care what you gave up and will continue to give up for your children!"

Let's pick apart what's wrong with that, shall we? First, we're supposed to profess to love that we have dark circles and presumably no time to apply eyeliner; love giving up late nights (or whatever it was we used to enjoy pre-motherhood, presumably) in favor of *Blues Clues* or whatever may represent the mind-numbing aspect of raising little ones (glitter crafts, say, or Play-Doh or Candy Land); and wear our teddy-bear–printed diaper bags as proudly as we once wore Coach.

> What's not healthy, for you or for your children, is to...feel compelled to view an unkempt ponytail not as merely a side effect of your busy new life, or as temporary until you have a chance to get to the stylist or the shampoo bottle, but as a *badge of honor.*

I know, I know: Isn't that really just another way of saying, *I love my new life?* Isn't it a good thing to embrace your changed circumstances? Heck, *didn't you want this baby*, for heaven's sake? Of course you did, and of course it's a good idea, and healthy, to embrace change. What's not healthy, for you or for your children, is to leap so far into it that you feel compelled to view an unkempt ponytail not as merely a side effect of your busy new life, or as temporary until you have a chance to get to the stylist or the shampoo bottle, but as a *badge of honor.*

Myth-to-reality

Reject any message, sentiment, or slice of peer pressure you suspect is telling you how you should feel about motherhood—particularly if the "should" is something that rings utterly false to you. Mothers receive the message—and not just from icky Facebook memes—that we are meant to be proud of giving up on ourselves (from decent haircuts and jeans that fit to showers and eyeliner) to give all to our kids. But I believe a lot more pride should lie in being able to *be a mother* while also *hanging on to ourselves.*

Sacrifice when you are a parent is a normal state of being. But *complete self-sacrifice* for its own sake, or in service to the mistaken belief that our children need us to sacrifice for them, is a bad wagon to hitch yourself to.

How to Ditch the Myths and Be the Mom You Are

Forget false Facebook status lines, and leave aside the sentiments expressed in Hallmark cards. The reality of hanging on to yourself is going to require some good old-fashioned honesty and real-world thinking.

You don't, contrary to popular belief, have to lose yourself in motherhood to be "good" at it. It's the opposite: holding on to who you are, I believe, makes you a better mother in the long run—and the long run is what being a Mean Mom is all about. Prescriptions for taking the real road:

+ **Work, in some way.** I always happened to be a working mother, so you may say (go ahead, say it) that I'm biased in favor of working. But bear with me. It's much, much easier to lose track of yourself when you don't work, when your whole job is your baby—and later, your child. But don't think I'm down on stay-at-home moms—I'm not. I'm half of one myself, given my work-at-home-but-only-when-they're-in-school status. Let me redefine what I mean by work: It can be a full-time job that you either didn't want to or couldn't, for practical or financial reasons, give up; it can be a reimagined part-time job; it can be a freelance business; it can be involvement with a community group, the PTA, or school board; it can be taking over your family's finances or helping to organize the business matters of family or friends. It can pay handsomely or not at all (though paying work is preferable, if you ask me!). You are within your rights to become very upset with me about this, but I refuse to back down: when I see a mother who seriously does nothing else but care for her child (and it's actually rare, especially if you take a look at my expansive list of "work" possibilities above), I see a mother who has no other place to put her energy, her hopes, her dreams, her talents, and her *everything else* but into parenting her child.

+ **Read books and magazines that have nothing to do with being a mother.** Okay, so I am admittedly devoted (some might call it demonically so) to my issues of the *New Yorker*. To me, allowing them to pile up unread, or for my long-standing subscription to go unfulfilled, would be like setting aside a piece of myself I wasn't willing to set aside. It can be very, very easy—seductive, really—to read only parenting books and magazines, if anything at all. But I maintain it's dangerous for you (and, not to beat the same drum over and over, for your child). It doesn't have to be about reading, but about something that's about you—that was, in a sense, part of *you*.

+ **Date your husband.** Do I do this? Um, not so much, not in the traditional sense of "dating." In the years we've been parents, my husband and I have become excellent jugglers of babies and toddlers and kids, of home details and cooking and shopping, of earning money. But that means we rarely go out on what anyone could reasonably call a "date." That said, I'm not all about "you must have a regular Friday night sitter/date or your marriage will falter and your kids will suffer." I'm about *what works for you?* That could be an inviolable, old-fashioned date-night-with-sitter situation. Or it could be, like my husband and me, a standing joke about how we celebrate our anniversary, on average, about nine months after the fact. Dating your husband or partner could mean something as simple as making an effort to *require* your children (once they're out of diapers, that is) to let you two talk over dinner. (Or even, now and then, not eating dinner with the kids!) It could be something as simple as shooing the tots away from the weekend breakfast table so you can have a second or third cup of coffee together without wiping chins and peeling bananas. Or it could be making a ritual of sending them to bed on a reliable schedule so you have those precious hours between their bedtime and yours to reclaim the couch, the TV remote, or whatever part of the house the two of you can relax in. For more on that, see below...

+ **Send your kids to bed. No, really. Do it.** I love my kids, I truly do. I enjoy seeing them do their kid things, wrinkle their brows as they read or play a computer game, figure out how to use a Nerf ball and an overturned side table as a basketball court, and so on. They're delightful, energetic, smart. And I don't spend all day with them, not usually, so you'd think I would want to stretch out bedtime and hang out with them every second I could. And yet I don't. And it's not just because, you know, they're kids and they get tired—and I long ago realized the value a good night's sleep has in affecting a child's health and well-being (not to mention his mood): it's because I get to a certain point, and I *need* my parent switch to move to "off." Think of when the quittin' time whistle blows and the guys in the quarry (remember *The Flintstones*?) dash off, free at last, with the whole evening ahead. Barring a special night, a party, or most weekends, we plan ahead to get the kids bundled off to bed by 8:00 p.m. They don't necessarily have to go to sleep (unless we've identified that they're seriously shot and need more shut-eye), but they do have to get out of our hair. It's not as though we're busting open champagne and slow-dancing in the living room. Sometimes we don't even talk much to each other. Sometimes it's solely the silence that we need, and certainly that I need. When I say "quittin' time" for the day's parenting, I'm not saying you should stop being a parent; that never happens (and you may, like we did, have a five-year-old who routinely has nightmares about bees that keeps you on duty). But I am saying you need that switch to slide to "off" so you can just...be...you.

+ **Buy yourself stuff you like.** Listen, I'm as frugal as the next gal. No, scratch that; I'm *way* more frugal than many of the next gals. Can't help it—it's inbred in me by a grandmother who sewed her own clothes and a mom who tore Brillo pads in half. (Seriously, though? That's actually a good idea. Brillo tends to rust out before it's used up, and half works as well as whole, so there's a tip you can take to the bank.) But. *But.* Whatever your budget allows, you should buy things that are just for you, like a lipstick or a DVD of one of those movies you feel you should own because you can watch it over and over (for me, that would be *When Harry Met Sally* or *Casablanca*). Or really swank wine glasses. Or a scarf. The list is naturally endless, but I hope you get the point: too many moms get such a (misfired) high off total self-sacrifice, and that just can't be good. Why should your child have nicer boots than you? No, really. Why? When I see a four-year-old with authentic Ugg boots while her mom is wearing Payless knockoffs, I shake my head with sadness.

+ **Take care of yourself physically.** I hope you're sensing a pattern here. Hanging on to yourself means taking care of yourself as best you can when your time and energy are so easily eaten up. Be sure you exercise, in whatever way works for you. Don't eat half-chewed chicken tenders for lunch. I tell you, when I let the day get away from me and end up glomming down half of my son's uneaten peanut butter and jelly sandwich, I feel like the mom who's put herself firmly in second (or third, or fourth) place. But when I serve the kids their lunch and then make myself a nice turkey sandwich, on the kind of roll they don't typically like, with maybe some hummus or a few slices of avocado, and some picante provolone to perk things up, I feel like...well, like *me*.

So, a final thought on hanging on to yourself: Motherhood is a huge upheaval. *Huge* doesn't even cover it; I'm not sure there's a huger word than *huge*, but imagine there is, and use that word to describe the shift from You to You-as-a-Mom. It can feel, if you buy into the myths, as though motherhood should or could be a seismic but utterly welcome upheaval in the life of a woman, a calling akin to sainthood, an immediate transformation into selfless perfection, or the hardest job on the planet.

But if you hold on to whatever version of yourself you had come to like and rely on before you became a mother, the seismic shift can be, if not welcome all the time, at least manageable and ultimately even rewarding—such as when it helps you uncover reserves of strength and love you didn't know you had. If you hang on to yourself, you'll realize you never quite cared to be a saint anyway and that being selfless isn't all it's cracked up to be (plus, kids do better with real women as their mothers, not angels with wings and saints in sackcloth). And if you hang on to yourself, you'll see there are many hard and rewarding jobs in the world. Motherhood is just one of them.

[3]

Mean Mom Manifesto #3:
Start as You Mean to Go On.

About a year before our son was born, friends of ours had their first child, a daughter. This couple set out quite deliberately to have their child and were thrilled both at how quickly they got pregnant and how good they felt about their beautiful new arrival. They expressed—without a trace of irony—how they believed this child chose them; they *wanted* her and set out to have her, to create her from the spirit and deep connection they felt between them as a couple (seriously, they're very normal people!).

I relate this in part to exemplify that they were, and still are, the most eager, earnest, and well-meaning of parents—not unlike many couples of this and the last generation. At the time—and this is relevant to the tale—they lived in a tiny apartment in Manhattan's East Village. By most localities' standards it was tiny, that is; for a trendy New York City 'hood, that it had two separate rooms tipped it to the enviable side of the scale, especially for young professionals.

As this hopeful, earnest, happy couple accepted gifts and gathered essentials for their baby-to-be, they began stowing the new stuff in their small-but-super-cool apartment's bedroom—a crib, car seat, bouncy seat, stroller. They figured, being by then seasoned Manhattanites, that it wouldn't be necessary to move out of the East Village or out of the city entirely; like generations of dedicated city dwellers before them, they reasonably figured they'd simply contract their own and their baby's stuff to fit into their apartment, to re-jigger the way they lived so that two could become three without a panicked flight to three bedrooms and a bath-and-a-half elsewhere. Their plan was to move their own bed into the living area, and reserve the bedroom for the baby and her stuff, in part so their infant would have a quiet place to sleep, and in part so her toys and things wouldn't be underfoot in the living area.

Makes sense. Except for what happened next: When they brought home their sweet, tiny baby girl, they kept her with them all the time, what with round-the-clock nursing, soothing, changing—not to mention a typical overeducated-new-parent anxiety, plus a very natural desire to gaze at their newborn's incredible face as much as possible. The baby started out her life nestled between her parents in their bed. And there she stayed. Until she was—wait for it—nearly eight years old!

And the bedroom, that precious slice of Manhattan square footage? Yeah, never got used, except as a storage space (and I'll bet the crib, like many a why-did-I-buy-this-anyway treadmill or exercise bike, was ultimately repurposed into a handy, if bulky, clothes hanger). So of course on the face of it, this seems silly, right? The fact that they were *not using* a whole entire room in their apartment. But even if they'd been in that four-bedroom suburban manse, it would have been worth this cautionary tale.

Hang on! I know what you're thinking. You think I'm about to launch into a diatribe about how co-sleeping is a bad idea. *I am not!* For the record—and please read this sentence twice before composing an indignant letter—I am *not* against co-sleeping, though it wasn't what we opted to do. I *am* in favor of parents first **figuring out** and then **sticking to** what works for them, rather than winging it.

Because when you wing too many aspects of parenting, you fall into the trap of thinking that changing stuff (such as extracting a school-age child from your bed) is *just so hard.* You fall prey to fear—fear of tantrums, say, if you take away a pacifier long past the time you think a pacifier should be plugging up your child's mouth, or fear of reprisals if you insist on at least a spoonful of peas alongside that hot dog.

> Because when you wing too many aspects of parenting, you fall into the trap of thinking that changing stuff (such as extracting a school-age child from your bed) is *just so hard.*

So, welcome to **Mean Mom Manifesto #3: Start as You Mean to Go On.** Parenting requires nothing if not bravery, and if you don't make the tough choices from early on (such as when you decide where the baby will sleep), you'll only kick the can down the road and find it harder to make tough choices when the stakes are much higher, such as when you have to decide if letting your thirteen-year-old go solo with friends to a rock concert is acceptable to you.

Nothing to Fear but Fear Itself

Fear is never a good fallback position when it comes to parenting. Does it go without saying that a Mean Mom doesn't fear? That was a trick question: a Mean Mom *does* feel fear—but she does it ("it" being the hard stuff) anyway. Too often, new parents operate with more than a little twinge of fear when they have a child, especially a first child. This is of course understandable. Heck, it happened to me, though thankfully it got fixed. What was I afraid of? Naps! Oh my, but those scared me.

When my older son was a newborn and we were home together, I got pretty good at some stuff—he was a champion nurser, so beyond the first thorny days of supply (not enough) and demand (too much!), we fairly quickly settled in to a nice nursing routine. It was winter, and I became, by necessity, competent at getting my boy quickly wrapped up in his bunting (quickly, that is, before he either had a blowout poop or it was time to feed him again) and nestled into his stroller so we could go for our chilly, boredom-busting daily walks. But when it came to consolidating those newborn-era catnaps into something resembling a schedule? Couldn't figure it out. And when I even *considered* the idea of putting him in his crib for a nap? It just seemed so...scary.

I know, right?! Afraid of a little baby (or, in my son's case, a very big baby). What did I think might happen? He'd pop up and demand another stroller nap, or a ride in his baby swing, while I tiptoed around afraid he'd wake up before he'd gotten a restful sleep? Well, yes, that *is* what I was afraid of. I want to be clear here, that there's nothing wrong with a baby having a series of catnaps all day long, schedule free. *If* that's what you, the mom, are comfortable with. I was stuck in a bind because I had identified that I *wanted* to work toward a predictable nap schedule. I just avoided trying it, afraid it wouldn't work. What "cured" me of my fear was my nanny, Maggie, whom I'd hired to care for the baby when I returned to work after three months. On my first or second day back on the job, when I called home, Maggie answered in a whisper. "Why are you whispering?" I asked. "Is he sleeping?"

"Yes," she answered. "He's in the crib."

"How did you get him to sleep in the crib?!" I asked, for some reason in a loud stage whisper, as if my boy could hear me from my office across town.

"He seemed sleepy," she said matter-of-factly, "so I put him down."

And there you are: a simple, straightforward answer—he seemed sleepy, so I put him down—and my fear evaporated. On my next day off, I tried it. Sure enough, as Maggie had related, I could identify the times he looked loopy enough to need a rest and pop him into the crib with a reassuring pat *right then.*

Had I remained fearful of trying? Those early months, even years, might have gone very differently for me because—for me, at least—being able to predict naps was a crucial piece of my mommy sanity. But once I realized, with the help of our dear Maggie, that I didn't really have anything to fear by laying down the nap law (or just laying down the baby!), I grew confident.

That's what I mean about choice, choosing those things that feel important or nonnegotiable to you, figuring out what your ideal scenario is and working from there to reach that point. And if you feel the fear? You do it anyway. I was (silly, but true) afraid of putting my baby down for a nap, thinking, "Well, *this* will never work!", but once I was presented with direct evidence that I really didn't have anything to fear, and I tried it, I realized that facing fear was not only a good move in the short term, but also could be instructive in the long term.

Picking Your Best Path

Let me explain: When you don't start out doing what you feel in your heart of hearts is the best approach in a given situation, or that best matches your lifestyle, you can find yourself stuck in a situation that makes you sad, frustrated, angry, or unsatisfied. You may end up feeling that it's impossible to break yourself out of the situation, thinking, "Well, this is the way it's going to be."

The friends I mentioned at the start of this chapter? They didn't set out to co-sleep, necessarily; they weren't committed to that option. They didn't *plan* for it, nor did they necessarily *want* it to go on as long as it did. Naturally, my first clue that they didn't intend to co-sleep for the long haul, or even that far into the first year, was that they, you know, *bought a crib*. But I actually have more concrete evidence that they rued their non-decision decision. *Because they told me so.*

When I got pregnant, these friends shared that they got the crib and set it up in the room because they wanted, they planned, to put their daughter in there someday. When *they* wanted to. When *they* decided they'd like to have their bed back. *If you want your baby in your bed for a long time, that's fine,* they told me. *But if we had it to do again, we'd start her in the crib sooner.*

Beginning with the baby

The whole idea of starting as you mean to go on suggests new parenthood, right? It actually can be applied all through your child's life, but just to be fair, let's start with the infants. Newsflash: Babies are awesome. In the actual, dictionary definition of "awesome," which is less the way Barney Stinson on *How I Met Your Mother* might use it, and more in terms of "inspiring awe." Awe, as my high school English teacher Ms. Richman liked to tell us, is really more like *fear* than like *wow*. So, yeah. Babies do often strike fear in the hearts of the uninitiated.

Think back to when those briskly efficient maternity nurses actually gave you your day- or days-old child and let you take him or her home. You didn't have to pass a test or anything (not including the buckle-him-into-the-car-seat test, which I failed miserably, and which the nurses re-did for us anyway). Remember that feeling? You knew you'd do anything it took to get the baby to just...do what a baby is meant to do. Namely, eat or sleep, depending on whether he'd recently eaten (in which case, he should sleep), or recently woke up (in which case, *why won't he eat*?!).

Babies can be scary, messy, confusing, and very, very demanding. You're in love, yes, and you probably have flashes of pure confidence. You know what I mean: the baby feeds really well then burps one of those from-deep-within belches, and you think, "I am so freaking good at this. He's been alive now for one whole week!"

But at the same time you're often on shaky, shifting ground, and that's scary. When he doesn't burp, or can't settle down to sleep and is inching toward meltdown status, it's hard to see past it. Pretty soon the irrational thought (which you only realize much later was quite so irrational) pops up that this particular stage, this thorny patch, will never, ever end, and it overpowers you. Pretty soon you'll do anything to change this scary thing that seems never-ending. And before you can say, "We're out of diapers!" congratulations! It's a pattern!

This weird vortex you descend into, in which every moment with your new baby has such great portent, has an awful lot to do with your own sleep deprivation. How can it not? When you're only sleeping in twenty- to thirty-minute snatches, you quickly start to feel as though you're living inside a Dali painting, complete with dripping clocks. There's a reason sleep deprivation is used as a form of torture.

Whatever the reason—sleep deprivation, the myopic vision

typical of new parents—many of us end up acting from a place of fear, and not out of a plan, not out of *starting as you mean to go on*.

Let me be clear that, in the brand-spanking-new-newborn period, that kind of reaction is (a) normal, (b) predictable, and (c) probably adaptive. If you didn't focus so intently on the here and now...well, I think you have no choice *but* to focus on the here and now, because when you're in the midst of your first experience with your own newborn, there only *is* a here and now. Every minute brings something new, and every other minute (or thereabouts) brings something scary. Momentous? Every hour or so. And so it goes for the first little while. Days, weeks, months.

Hold on there! Months? Nope—it's time to take stock now. Are you starting as you mean to go on? Are you doing something—feeding a certain way, scheduling or not scheduling naps, holding and rocking to sleep or not—because it's what you *want* to do, with an outcome that you think you would be reasonably contented with? Or are you still shooting straight from the hip—still acting out of that awe/fear mode? If you haven't broken out of that pure reaction mode, you're more likely to do the kinds of things that, like the friends whose story I told at the start of this chapter, may lead you to a rueful comeuppance. *What the heck did we do that we ended up with a six-year-old kicking the bejeezus out of our kidneys every night?*

While early on, reaction mode is adaptive, so is experimentation. I bought a front-baby-carrier thinking it would be fantastic to not be tied to a stroller to get around town, but I found that it only hurt my shoulders, and that my son was happy being able to look out at the world rather than be on my chest—something I wouldn't have known if I hadn't tried. Same goes with things like co-sleeping or whether you'll nurse exclusively, pump milk to use bottles sometimes, or supplement with or use formula. But also as with reaction mode, experimentation has to end eventually, as you settle on what works for you and...you got it, continue as you mean to.

There's harsh, and then there's just hard

Starting as you mean to go on can seem hard, but it's not, or doesn't have to be, harsh. Many of us may have been raised by parents who, like Betty Draper, the willow-waisted '60s mom of *Mad Men*, believed you could spoil an infant with an excess of cuddling (but not with an excess of blowing smoke rings over the crib, apparently). And it may be that, in reaction, we became a bit too laid-back. My contention is that you don't have to make a stark choice between Ice Queen Betty Draper (who locked her daughter in a closet for some misbehavior or other) and the kind of parent who ends up too afraid to even frown at a child who's caught with his hand in the cookie jar, so to speak. We feel, correctly, that Mrs. Draper's methods were too harsh, but in reaction we may just be avoiding what's hard—or what's "mean"—but still right.

Here's what I mean by the difference between *harsh* and *hard:*

Harsh: Letting a newborn cry with hunger in a rigid belief that babies should only be fed on a four-hour schedule.

Hard: Gradually moving an infant *toward* a feeding schedule that makes sense for you.

Harsh: Allowing a baby who *should* be sleeping to "cry it out" at the tender age of two months.

Hard: Figuring out what sleep-teaching method is right for your family—and then actually doing it, for the sake of everyone's health and sanity.

Harsh: Requiring a three-year-old to be seen and not heard in a restaurant or at a family holiday table.

Hard: Working out ways to let your growing child know what sort of behavior is expected of her in different situations, tailored to her age.

So, it's easy to reject *harsh*. But it's not so simple to adopt the *hard*.

It's hard to set and stick to rules. Hard to create a workable schedule (either with a baby if that's what you want, or later on with growing children). Hard to be the heavy, hard to see the future. Hard to imagine that, sometimes, you're not going to be your child's most favorite person in the world.

And that's when we end up slipping into behaviors—patterns, really—that feel like the right idea at the time because they provide immediate comfort for the baby and immediate relief for us. Now, I'm not saying you shouldn't provide comfort, far from that. (I envy what Betty Draper's obstetrician called her "remarkably resilient figure," but I don't envy her reluctance, probably born of how she herself was raised, to cuddle her children.) But providing comfort without setting yourself up for all sorts of thorny

> Starting as you mean to go on is all about resisting the pull of the path of least resistance.

problems or tough-to-break patterns later is where the Mean Mom converges with the good mom.

Starting as you mean to go on is when you choose how you want things to turn out generally: "I want a child who is a joy to take to restaurants," or, "I want a child who respects me, his grandparents, his teachers," or even something simple like, "I want a baby who can sleep in his own space all night long," and then set out to create situations where those goals can, eventually, be met.

Starting as you mean to go on is all about *resisting the pull of the path of least resistance.*

Let me be more specific—because you'll see I'm talking about pretty specific things, like rocking a baby every time he needs to go to sleep, lying in a preschooler's bed night after night (and ending up with a sore back and a kid who *still* can't sleep without you), or popping in a pacifier long after pacifiers are generally needed. Again, if these are things you honestly don't mind for the long term, then that's great. But many times, for many parents, these are temporary solutions we grab at for the short term, and we either don't think about what's down the road at all, or we think that we can just *change it later*, like we can change a sheet with baby vomit on it. The truth is, though, that taking the path of least resistance now sets you on the path of incredibly-hard-to-change later.

A few examples of what I mean by path-of-least-resistance parenting:

You rock your baby to sleep every night, or multiple times a night, long after she really needs that kind of attention. Listen, I'm not an ogre; I loved nursing my babies all the time, but particularly at night. There is nothing as sweet as a drowsy and milk-drunk baby, with those fluttering eyelashes and that flushed skin. But I was always careful to put my baby boys down when they were done eating and sleepy, but not dead asleep, because somewhere in my reptilian brain, I knew that if I got started on that path, I'd be one of those moms who ends up sleeping on the floor of her three-year-old's room, and I didn't want that to happen. Babies—and this was a lightbulb moment for me, when I discovered this—don't *know* how to fall asleep on their own; they don't necessarily grow into it (though some undoubtedly do) the way they grow teeth or hair. You have to teach them. And rocking teaches them that they can't possibly fall asleep without being rocked.

The start as you mean to go on approach: No, it's not throwing a wide-awake baby into his crib in his dark and desolate room all by himself. Instead, it's gently winding down toward bedtime, then putting your sleepy, content, but still sort of awake baby into whatever you call his bed, and saying whatever constitutes "night night."

You drive around the block to get him to nap. Hasn't there been a car commercial like this? Of course, the people who dream up advertisements for family vehicles would love it if you opted for their SUV or minivan because it seemed like a nice place to spend every afternoon at 3:00 p.m. I also understand that there are a few infants who are...let's be charitable and call them "hard to soothe" or "challenging," and for those babies, a ride in a gently rumbling vehicle, or a stroller trip, or time spent in a baby swing, is the *only* thing that stops the tears and the wails. But that should be short-lived. There's just no reason that an eighteen-month-old should be taken for a gas-guzzling tour of the neighborhood every time it's sleepy time.

The start as you mean to go on approach: Er, is it too simple—or too smugly mean—to just say, *stop it already*? But really, even said more kindly, that's basically what you need to do, unless you *honestly* don't mind breaking away from a lunch date or your own routine in the house to drive your toddler to shut-eye. Because what you're doing when you persist is twofold: One, going back to what I've said before, you're missing opportunity after opportunity to teach your child to fall asleep on her own. But two, you're putting yourself not just second but out of the picture entirely. *You*, or what you would like to do with your day, or how you'd like to spend your child's naptime, don't matter. What matters is buckling a crying, tantruming, obviously overtired tot into a car seat and taking a cruise. Each kid is different in terms of how much daytime sleep he or she needs (though they *all* need plenty of sleep, full stop) or will tolerate, but your best bet is to learn to identify your own child's "I might be getting tired here" cues and settle him or her down *then*, rather than waiting until it's too late to settle.

You have a seemingly unbreakable pacifier habit. A few weeks back, I was shopping at Target, which is both a necessity and a source of entertainment for me. Anyway, as I was coming around a corner I heard a woman saying, "No, no, we're *not* going to look at the binkies! We're not even going down that aisle!" What I saw was a family with a child who looked to be about five, with a pacifier in his mouth. Now, I get the pacifier thing, I really do (my kids loved 'em, and so did I). And I am not judging anyone who thinks, for whatever reason, that it's okay for a five-year-old to still, not only use a pacifier, but also actively want to shop for a new pacifier. I don't *understand* it, but I'm not *judging* it.

I wouldn't even be sharing this anecdote if the parents in question weren't so obviously annoyed and frustrated by their child's binkie habit. If they had been cool with it ("Hey, son, let's hit the binkie aisle!"), I'd have found it merely odd, but not a good illustration of my point. Thing is, though, this mom *clearly*—trust me, I saw it in person—didn't want her son to still be a sucker. Seemed to me that somewhere along the line, she'd taken the path of least resistance and just let the habit go on. And on.

The start as you mean to go on approach: All bad habits that you want to help your child break, or, for that matter, good habits that you want to reinforce, take forethought. It's really not that hard to axe a pacifier habit, if that's what you want to do. You just have to decide that that's what you'll do, without being afraid that any resistance (which you may get, but you may just as likely be surprised *not* to get) will go on so long or be so onerous that you'll be compelled to give up (and end up discussing binkie buying in Target with your kindergartner). That's like the parents who let a toddler or preschooler's unruly behavior in a restaurant go (he's just a baby, right?), and then forget that he's now six years old, or seven, and not a baby anymore, and so shouldn't be unruly in a restaurant.

You never did manage a sitter (even your willing—and free!—mom) because the separation anxiety thing was just too much. There are developmental points in a child's first year—the first being at around seven to eight months—when your baby realizes that (surprise!) when you go away, you still exist. And if you still exist, then he can miss you. Which often makes him cry. It's a simple progression, but it never feels simple when you try to leave a child with a raging case of separation anxiety with someone else. If you could translate a baby's separation-anxiety-induced screaming into English, it would go something like this: "How dare you leave me! What are you doing over there in the other room or not even in the house? Having fun with some other baby? *Will you ever come back*?!" So, yeah, the reaction is a potent, strong (and loud!) argument for *not* leaving. But if not now, when? What many parents do, afraid of that screaming mess of the separation-anxious baby, is *not* leave. Not now, not ever. Oops. You gotta go sometime.

The start as you mean to go on approach: Just go. No, not to Europe for the summer, but out for dinner with your husband, coffee with your friend, even the other room for heaven's sake.

Because here's what happens when you do actually leave: Before long, presuming your substitute caregiver is a caring one (or your baby is safe and content playing with his toys on the floor), your baby will quit screaming, distracted by anything from a feeding to a toy to a tickle to just *time*. And here's the other thing: You come back. And when you come back, he realizes, "Oh, okay. This isn't so bad. Sure, I'd prefer her to be my constant companion, but Grandma/the sitter/daycare provider is okay, and she comes back!"

I want to be clear that, when I talk about *starting as you mean to go on*, I'm not just talking about nap skills and pacifier habits. That's just the beginning. The common and modern parental fear of breaking bad habits, like the drive-by nap or the pacifier in Target at age five, is an approach that can easily spool out into something worse if you let it go on. Even if you work out all those first-year kinks, you can still get into trouble when you drop the reins and make ongoing parenting decisions based on:

1. **Fear.** This bears repeating, so here goes: Too often, we avoid making changes (I hesitate to say "implementing rules," but there's that, too) because we're afraid that the resistance will be so stiff and painful that it will take, quite literally in our minds, *forever*. It never does. It sucks to sleep-train (if that's your plan), but it's usually over quickly when you follow through consistently with it. But if you *don't* do it for fear it'll be too hard or take too long, or if you give up too easily out of fear, well, it'll never happen.

2. **Unwillingness to see your child uncomfortable.** Even temporarily. No one wants a child to suffer on purpose, of course. But there's almost no getting around that if you are trying to break a pacifier habit, enforce a rule about bedtime, say *no* to before-dinner treats (if that's your thing), tell an eight-year-old that he can't buy the Wii game he just saw in the store, or your twelve-year-old that an iPhone is not in her immediate future, your child will feel that uncomfortable, "Hey, I'm not getting what I want!" feeling. But honestly, it's okay for a baby or child to feel uncomfortable. It doesn't last forever, and she learns from it—not only picking up your rules and values, but also discovering her own ability to cope with discomfort.

3. **Apathy.** Pure and simple, sometimes it's a cross between procrastination and path-of-least-resistance thinking that leads parents to put off all kinds of things. Take sleep training or nap-scheduling (if that's what you eventually *want*, remember) because it is, well, *easier* to scoop up the over-cranky toddler and drive him around the block than it is to bite the bullet and settle him down for a "real" nap. Or say you'd like, someday, to make just one meal for dinner, not an adults' dinner with a speedily prepared kids' meal. The sooner you set aside the apathy ("I can't stand the push back on the slow-cooker stew; I'll just give her plain noodles for tonight. Tomorrow I'll try..."), the sooner the kid realizes you're not a short-order cook. (And for the record, my mother made stew and I hated it—the foods *touched* each other, for

heaven's sake—but I ate it, just enough anyway, to satisfy my parents and my tummy.)

As with everything related to children, the older they get, the higher the stakes, because the more ingrained the patterns become, the more organized the resistance will be to efforts to change the goal lines. Again, I want to be clear that I'm talking not about *my* parenting prescriptions (or anyone else's, from so-called experts to bossy PTA moms to your nosy and opinionated sister-in-law). I'm talking about your *own* ideas of how you'd like things to turn out. Put simply, if you want your child to learn French, it ain't gonna happen if you don't speak the language around her (presuming you can *parlez-vous francais*, that is!).

Kids pick up a lot of habits; if you start as you mean to go on, the habits they pick up *in your home, under your influence* are at least ones you can be confident you want them to have, or won't be embarrassed that they have.

Where "Start as You Mean to Go On" Started

This particular Mean Mom Manifesto gelled a couple of years ago when two things happened that, while they at first seemed unrelated, served to drive home the same point. The first: a conversation I overheard in my younger boy's preschool classroom one day. A mom of one of my son's classmates was chatting with the teacher about how she was taking her daughter to the dentist; the five-year-old had a cavity. She said, "Well, I'm sure one problem is all the candy she eats! My mother-in-law fills her pockets with candy when I'm not looking." All I could think was this: *Okay, your mother-in-law fills the kid's pocket with sweets. And there's seriously nothing you can do about that? Is it out of your hands?* I get that sometimes relatives (grandparents, in particular) can be quite persistent in their efforts to spoil and treat the little ones in their lives.

Just right off the top of my head I came up with two solutions this mom could have employed to take back control of her daughter's candy intake (presuming, you know, that she wasn't happy with said intake, and I did make the presumption, given the way she bemoaned the trip to get the cavity filled, and the way she scapegoated her mother-in-law):

+ She could have told her mother-in-law (nicely, not so nicely, through her husband, in an email, via registered letter, whatever might have felt right) to *please not put candy in the kid's pocket.* She may have had to repeat that four or five (hundred) times, but it's not totally out of the realm of possibility to have at least *tried.*

+ She could have removed the candy from her daughter's pockets. Then she might have, as I do when large stashes of candy come my kids' way, picked through it for the worst stuff, tossed that, then saved the rest for treats to be doled out as, well, *treats.*

Difficult? Sure, depending on the whole mother-in-law, daughter-in-law dynamic. But is it harder to nip the candy habit in the bud now in the short-run, or harder to passively let it go and deal with the consequences, such as taking a five-year-old to the dentist? Or deal with a child who feels *entitled* to candy (now) and anything else that's blithely offered to her (later)?

And I'd argue that saying "no thanks, Mom" to the candy or dealing with an upset five-year-old is not nearly as hard to stomach doing now as what you might be faced with later, when the stakes are a lot higher than a pocketful of Jolly Ranchers. Which brings me to the second story that relates to the birth of the "start as you mean to go on" manifesto. Last year some time, I'd noticed, in some Facebook photos posted by a friend of my then-high-school-junior nephew, that some of the kids he'd gone to his junior prom with were drinking vodka in the limo (or at least posing with it for the photos). In casual conversation, I mentioned that fact to my sister. *Oh, yeah,* my sister said. *Some of those kids drink like fish.* So, okay, I get that kids drink; I get that they'll find out how to procure alcohol and drink it no matter what we say or do, as a broad general rule (though I'd still argue that setting clear rules and adding in a good dose of education might mitigate how much, or how early, they drink, but I digress).

I wasn't surprised that there was vodka in the prom limo. What surprised me was what my sister shared next: she said that another mom she knows lets her teens and their friends drink in the house. That same mom said, after she'd dropped off her daughter and two of her fifteen-year-old friends at a Sweet Six-teen party, "Oh, I know they had vodka in their water bottles, but what can I do?"

Sigh. So we're back to the candy-in-the-pocket (and even, if you follow the thread all the way back, the pacifier in Target).

What can you do? Oh, I don't know. You could, if you're the mom who knows there's vodka in your underage passengers' Poland Spring bottles, *turn the car around, drop off the other kids, and tell your child in no uncertain terms that this sort of behavior is unacceptable.* That's just one option.

The line between the candy and the vodka seemed very clear to me. Now, I'm not saying that the little girl in my son's class is going to start bringing water bottles filled with vodka to kinder-garten as a direct result of her mother's passivity about clearing her pockets of Grandma's Jolly Ranchers. But it's on the same continuum. I could imagine the mother throwing up her hands about the candy being the same kind of parent who'd say, "Let's just let them drink in our home with their friends when they're fifteen, because they're going to anyway, no matter what we do."

I don't agree.

Start as you mean to go on.

And please, don't throw up your hands.

[4]

Mean Mom Manifesto #4: Don't Follow the Parenting Pack.

Remember junior high?

Remember believing, down to your shoes (which were probably the wrong ones), that the cool girls had some sort of magic key to popularity? Remember how, in those days, those cool girls and the other kids who "followed" them set certain benchmarks for what clothes were fashionable, what skating rink was the "right" one for Friday night, or whether carrying a comb in your back pocket was the done thing, or if you should keep your hair implements in your Le Sportsac handbag?

Do you also remember how, once you got past all that stuff—as in, when you grew up—you got smart enough to leave that kind of peer-pressure minutiae behind? You should try to remember that now that you're a parent, because there's a new set of "cool girls" in town, and they're what I call The Parenting Pack. It's not *quite* the same as junior high (slightly less acne, for one thing, and most of us can drive to the mall whenever we want without relying on our moms), but there are times, I'm sure you've all found, that The Parenting Pack is telling you that there's a "right" way to be a mom, and most definitely a "wrong" way, and it can be tough to drown it out.

The Parenting Pack, in other words, is a giant ball of mommy peer pressure, and to be a Mean Mom, this prescription—**Mean Mom Manifesto #4: Don't Follow the Parenting Pack**—is critical.

I'm not saying you have to be a square peg of a parent and completely fly solo in all your ideas and tenets about parenting, but you do have to embrace whatever shape your peg happens to be—square or round, trapezoid or octagonal. If most of the moms you see around you appear to be nice round pegs, and the parenting styles you know about appear to be nice and round, too, it can be tempting to force yourself into that opening. You can try, or try part of the round-hole (aka "popular") approach, but the moment something chafes or feels uncomfortable, discard it like the shoes that looked nice in the store but gave you blisters in real life.

> If you start out parenthood trying to follow the pack, you'll only end up exhausted and disoriented trying to keep up— and with a race that keeps changing course, to boot.

If you start out parenthood trying to follow the pack, you'll only end up exhausted and disoriented trying to keep up—and with a race that keeps changing course, to boot.

The "This Is How It Is" Police

Have you encountered the "this is how it is" police yet? And you thought maternity-ward nurses were tough! From the moment you become a parent, it seems, the "this is how it is" police begin to issue directives. Oh, it's not that anyone hands you an actual printed list of to-dos and never-dos; you absorb it from the prevailing culture. Some depends on where you live—the circles you run in, as the expression goes—but much of it derives from the general parenting zeitgeist.

This is what you do during maternity leave: you find your baby playgroup and make sure you have the right kind of stroller.

This is how you grocery shop with toddlers: you bring snacks and a germ-proof padded liner for the shopping cart.

This is how you do playdates: you bring snacks and kvetch about husbands and mothers-in-law.

This is how you do a trip to the park: you bring snacks. (I'm jesting. A little bit.)

Sometimes the "this is how it is" police can get more onerous than the notion that you can't possibly venture too far from your own home without a pocketbook filled with baggies of Goldfish crackers. (How far *do* you live from town? If it's less than 25 miles, you can all survive without a snack. Can't you?) Sometimes it's about playing with or paying attention to your kids (you sit on the floor and play Candy Land whenever asked, right?). Sometimes it's about your approach to safety (you'd never, and I mean *never* just release your child and his friend into the backyard, would you? Without standing there and watching? *Right?*)

I honestly don't think my own mother got any memos, real or perceived, from the "this is how it is" police. She parented the way she felt was right, rejecting pressure, of which little likely existed anyway, to do things in a way that might fit in. She gets a good deal of credit for this, in my opinion, but I also maintain that she had it easier, given that the chorus (again, not *actual* voices, but amorphous and powerful cultural ones) was much more muted back then.

One of the main issues with the pressure you might feel from The Parenting Pack is how it can make you feel like a bad mom if you're not careful. Let's say you didn't sign up your daughter for hip-hop dance *just because you didn't care to add another activity to the schedule.* The Parenting Pack might make you feel—with their seemingly selfless willingness to find another day to squish in that hip-hop class—that you're not living up to the Good Mom image.

And even if you can duck the bad-mother guilt on that front, "this is how it is" can cut deeper when it becomes this sense that you should choose a *system,* follow the *rules,* and, well, *fit in.* You get a lot of back-patting credit when you fit in, when you parrot the party line on everything from how you give birth to how you feed your baby, to how you "socialize" her, to what sort of birthday parties or holiday presents you offer, to what activities you enroll your child in (before he's figured out for himself what extracurricular pursuits he actually likes).

Conversely, you're likely to get a lot of stink-eye sideways glances when you admit cheerfully that you didn't—to use just one example—buy your child a Christmas gift "from Santa" until he was actually old enough to know what that meant.

The "this is how it is" police (really, it's not so much "police" as it is "prevailing winds," but police reflects the siren-blaring urgency some of us feel at some points in parenting) creates a sense, when we're not careful to reject it and plumb our own instincts for the answers that are right for us, that *following the pack is best for our children.* So there! Do it this way not because you want to fit in with the other moms you see! No, that would be so shallow! *Do it this way because if you don't, you're shortchanging your child.*

And nothing puts the fear of God—or the fear of the mom in the minivan next to you who seems to be doing all the correct, right-in-line, *how it is* things— in a new or newish mother than the thought that she might be doing wrong by her child. But if you hear nothing else I'm

> When you're not doing what's right for *you,* you're not doing what's right for *your children.*

saying, get this: When you're not doing what's right for *you,* you're not doing what's right for *your children.* With some caveats, of course; I'm not saying that if it feels right for you to drink red wine while sitting up on the roof with your lover, watching your children set fires in the backyard, well, obviously...

What not following the pack looks like

When you don't follow the pack, guess what you have to follow instead? Yes! Your instincts! Dig around there—you have them. You do. It takes a little work, but only you can figure out how parenting feels and works best for you and your family.

Nothing works to illustrate the point like a few good real-life examples, so here are some ways I've ventured off the grid, sang my own tune, so to speak. And it's not only me—I polled some friends and colleagues and realized that even though many of us may remain silent when the *this is how it's done* police sirens start wailing, there are plenty of us digging around for those instincts and working out our own *how it's done* rules. Here's a sampling of areas in which following The Parenting Pack may lead you in the wrong (that is to say, unsatisfied) direction, and how I deviated from the pack mentality:

The baby-care cabal

Especially when you're a first-time mother, choosing the so-called style of baby care that feels right can be fraught. Try not to fall under the spell that what *appears* to be most virtuous is also the most right.

Let's say all of your friends who recently had babies adopted an attachment-parenting approach—wearing their babies in slings, feeding on demand, co-sleeping. If that appeals to you, do it if you want, but not *because* anyone makes you feel compelled to do so, or less than a good mom if you don't. (Also, be aware that, as with any style of baby care, you can pick and choose from *within* types. So, you can breastfeed, but not on demand. You can wear your baby in a sling, but not co-sleep.) If your aunt—who you otherwise adore—tells you you're doing your baby wrong by not strictly scheduling feedings, and that feels somehow off to you, feel free to reject (kindly) her suggestions.

I nursed each of my babies for more than a year, but the attachment parenting people might have frowned on me for not feeding on demand. I tried it. It made me cry (not a joke). I felt panic rising on the one day that my then-two-week-old boy fell into a pattern of snack-and-release. *Am I ever going to get out of here? Button my shirt? Ever?!* I knew that wasn't going to work—for me. I finagled him back onto an every-three-hour schedule of boob-emptying feedings, and after that, we were both happier. I didn't co-sleep, because I'm not the greatest sleeper in the world to begin with (I'm not even always a fan of co-sleeping with my husband, to be honest, and don't worry, he knows and is not offended) and I needed my boundaries from my child.

Boundaries are the key, really. Decide what boundaries you need, and if you're deciding based on something you read, or something your friend did, or something that the bristling, bustling maternity ward nurse who tries to bully you into formula (or the La Leche League rep who does the opposite), scrap it and decide based on what feels right. I had to do what was right for me, and so do you—even if *right for you* seems awfully, well, *mean*. Get over it, be mean, be good for yourself first.

Playgroup peer pressure

Even though playgroups were *the* thing to do when I had infants, I skipped them. When I had my first child and was on maternity leave for three months, we lived in a New York City neighborhood in which I could find, if I looked, virtually any kind of food in the world (not to mention language) and also—again, had I looked—any kind of person. If I'd wanted another mom to have coffee with while our infants rolled around on a rug, or a group of moms to gossip with while we pushed the babies on swings in the park, I could have. But I didn't. And that suited me fine. First of all, that initial three months is total immersion time—it's baby boot camp, and for my baby and me to get to know each other and work out our kinks and jitters, we needed to be alone.

I'll put it this way: I missed being nearer my *closest* friends, or having a sister or a cousin, someone I already knew, in the same stage of life and motherhood as me, but I wasn't missing it quite enough to go looking for a substitute. I didn't really crave that kind of belongingness until much later, when my baby and I were swinging suburbanites, when I was working three days a week and had two days at home with a more fun, more mobile kid. Before that, seeking a passel of other mothers I felt like hanging out with seemed like more work than I had the brain space for. But as I said back then—and maybe now, too—playgroups were like the pre- pre- preschool of modern, hip, want-to-do-it-right parents. But I didn't believe my child needed socializing—or even *could* play—with other tots, so why would I get together with other moms and complain about my husband or that *I really shouldn't be eating this pound cake!* when what I really wanted to do was take a long walk in the neighborhood and take care of my errands and nurse my baby while we watched *30-Minute Meals with Rachael Ray*? But by contrast, had the prevailing wisdom been that new moms should go it alone—and not "waste time" in coffee klatches, or if the vogue was to keep your child away from the influence of other, possibly more germy, babies, but you felt that going it alone would destroy your last nerve as well as your last brain cell, then *that* would be the trend for you to buck.

Avoiding the Pack Mentality

WHAT YOU HEAR:	WHAT THE PACK-FOLLOWER MIGHT SAY:	WHAT THE MEAN MOM MIGHT SAY:
You don't breastfeed on demand?	Why? Should I worry about bonding if I don't? Oh, dear...	It didn't work for me. You?
You've *never* taken your baby to a music-and-movement class?	Well, not yet, but I'm trying to find one and in the meantime we have a half-hour of at-home tambourine-ing a day.	Ugh, just the idea of tambourines makes me itch. But he's developing quite a love for The Ramones!
What are you doing for her first birthday?	Still looking for the ideal spot; right now we're trying to get her to settle on a theme.	Birthday party? You mean, having the grandparents over for cupcakes and pizza?
How many preschools have you researched?	Four. Wait—is that too few? There *are* some in the next two towns over...	Two. The first one I checked out, and the one I decided on. Done!

The baby "class" circuit

In another sea change since many of our mothers had us, you can now take classes with your child practically from birth, from infant "music and movement" sessions to Gymboree and Mommy and Me. Where I live, this is just what you do (and if you're a working mother, you find the weekend class, or have your mother, your husband, or your baby-sitter take the child in your stead), but such classes didn't appeal to me. I tried Mommy and Me at our local library, but to be honest, our first several tries left me cold. I could never quite fit it into my schedule, for one thing. And for another, on the off chance you've never been to one of these classes, Mommy and Me involves stuff like maracas and tambourines, glue and glitter—four things I'm not a huge fan of. Interestingly, when I asked other moms I know who are well out of this stage, quite a chunk of them—in my thoroughly unscientific poll—admitted they, too, gritted their teeth as they were asked to "shake their sillies out." During the "craft" portion of the class, I was much more apt to sit with my boy in my lap and let him play with the glue bottle and "glue" pieces of snowman or sailboat wherever he fancied (which was often on the table itself, forget about the paper), while other moms around me were guiding little hands to create the perfect picture. I'm not sure if my son was having fun, but I know I wasn't.

It wasn't right for me, and later, when both my boys were in day care and did all their glue-and-glitter crafts and tambourine-banging songs while they were with someone other than me, I realized my instincts had been right. That stuff just isn't my bag, and squishing myself into doing it *because it was what the mom-pack was doing and therefore it must be right and necessary* would be as uncomfortable as squishing my body into control-top pantyhose, and thank heaven I don't have to do *that* any longer.

Finding "family" friends

Many new mothers, in a sheer, if understandable, panic that they need friends *for their babies*, hook up with every other new mother they see. Whereas a friend-criteria might once have been a similar taste in music and movies; aligned political, religious, or cultural views; or that you went to the same school, joined the same sorority, or survived the same boss, now that you have a child you are prone to alter your standard to this one, simple fact: *Is her child the same age as mine?* That's a fine criteria for, say, an online message board, where you might plug into the forum for moms of babies born in November of 2012 and share worries about pacifiers and potty training with anonymous, geographically scattered moms in the same general trenches. But what about you? Don't you still have needs for friends you can hang out with? Have a beer, a margarita, a chai latte, or some decaf coffee and fat-free pound cake with? You can't talk about the babies forever.

I actually did find our first real "other parent" friends using the kid-the-same-age logic and approached a couple pushing a stroller containing a girl who looked about our son's age at a garage sale. We were both eyeing the Little Tikes outdoor climbing toy. We hesitated, and they bought it. (They still have it, I think. After all, Little Tikes never dies; it just fades in the sun.) And we're still friends.

I may have approached initially because they looked like people we might have something in common with. But had we not actually ended up *having* anything in common, we wouldn't have remained friends. Interestingly, these days our children aren't that tight (a boy and a girl, at the wise old age of eight, aren't usually best buds), but we moms still are, because as it turns out, she and I both exist in that weird, hard-to-find hybrid of work at home/stay at home. My point is, the balance has shifted from kids-are-playdate-pals-so-parents-have-to-hang-out to parents are likely to invite each other to adult parties, at which *kids* have to go along and get along.

Child-care choices

Recently, I was chatting with a friend who just signed her two-year-old daughter up for a preschool/child-care place that my younger son also went to in his prekindergarten year. We compared notes on the pros and cons of the place. That the school's director has a sickly sweet kind of New-Agey approach and that the rooms are sort of cramped were on the con list. But on the pro side, it is *very* close to both of our homes. I told my friend how, on a day my younger son had an accident and I'd forgotten to re-supply his cubby with spare clothes, I could be there with a fresh set of sweats before they even got him cleaned off. For a working mother, that's priceless, and—I'm not afraid to admit this—it outweighs trying to attain the elusive "ideal" child-care spot.

Parents drive themselves nuts trying to find a Mary Poppins nanny or a day-care situation that treads that perfect line between loving and learning. I say ditch the search for perfection, and choose based on criteria that feel instinctually right for you, even if "right for you" means, as it did for me and later for my friend—"within a mile from home or work." While it's true that I would most assuredly *not* have picked a day care run by a chain-smoking ex-con who took in local kids to help support her rabid backyard pit bulls *just* because it was conveniently located on the next block, the fact is that the preschool I did choose was perhaps not the *very best* in all categories, but it was certainly plenty good enough.

Here's what I did: I trusted my instincts *over* the "reviews" of others. My thought process was: I visited this place, and it was fine. It was state licensed. It was clean. And my boy thrived there. Done.

I had done the same thing when it came to day-care choices earlier in my sons' lives. I didn't spend ages searching and second-guessing; I stopped once I'd found Good Enough. Shocking, but true. Mean, but true: the day care had to work *for me* before it would be the one I chose *for them*.

Toys-R-Not-Us

The Parenting Pack might give you the message that your child "needs" a lot of toys or, at the very least, that there's nothing you can do about the avalanche of primary-colored plastic that's about to hit your home. Not true! Thing is, if you *want* or *care to* own or have *room for* every piece of equipment or toy out there, then go for it. If it's not your bag, your child won't suffer.

There are people who don't believe me, but I swear this is true: The one and only toy I bought for my child, for the first four or five years of his life, was the Monkey Bed. I don't know its official name, or if it has one, but we called it the Monkey Bed. It was a small crib-like thing, and it came with three bouncing monkeys (basically, little rubber balls covered in orange, purple, and green felt with a monkey head, legs, and tail). You bounced the monkeys onto the crib/bed thing, and it sang (the bed sang, that is) "Three Little Monkeys Jumping on the Bed." (You know the song; you're welcome for the earworm.) I was in Babies R Us with my son looking for a gift for someone else, and saw the Monkey Bed. Something about it just tickled my fancy, so I bought it, and the boy *loved* it. So did his little brother, later.

Anyway, other than the Monkey Bed, I never bought a toy until the very first time my older boy got around to *asking* for something from Santa for Christmas. (For the record, he was six years old, and it was a trumpet. I don't know why, either.) My thought was, why would I buy them toys? Living in a small-ish apartment at first, I had a pathological fear of Toys Taking Over. We had a tiny collection of playthings to start with, all gifts from my baby shower. Thereafter, they'd get a few toys as gifts from grandparents and aunts and uncles. What more did they need really?

Pick-and-choose parties

I know a couple who, when their now-three-year-old turned one—admittedly a major event, a child's first birthday—hosted a budget-busting blowout at a fancy catering place, one that would be a stretch to host a wedding, for many people. I couldn't help but think: Where do they go from there? If they keep up at that rate, they'll have to rent out Tahiti for the girl's nuptials—and I mean the actual island nation!

That birthday brouhaha is an extreme example of the lengths some parents go to celebrate their children's birthdays, at an age when they (the kids, that is) don't much notice. In my opinion, first birthdays in particular are mostly (and rightly) about the parents. You invite nearest and dearest to mark the date on which you can say: We survived the first year intact! And you take pictures of your adorable baby, his double chin bisected by the elastic band of his party hat, and his cheeks smeared with chocolate and/or whipped cream.

To my mind, for this and the next few birthdays, not a lot more is needed. Which does not mean that you can't go all out and book a party with more panache than your average at-home gig, if you so choose. What I'm getting at here is avoiding the pressure of believing you *have* to, for example, invite all twenty-four kids in the day-care group or preschool class to a party if that's not something that'll make you, or your wallet, happy.

I may be going out on a total Mean-Mom limb here, but so what if everyone else did it? Don't feel you have to reciprocate and host a party that you can't afford (or don't fancy having if you can fit it into your budget) just because your child has been invited to a clutch of them. When your child is one, two, three—who is the party for? For them, or for you to either show you "care," or make a point to The Parenting Pack that you're doing the done thing?

Ballet and soccer and violin, oh, my!

Both of my boys play soccer (and I use the term "play" loosely; the little guy seems to have some actual promise, while my older son is mostly in it for the camaraderie and the Munchkins—and to me, either one is fine). I feel grateful that we found a local league that caters to the goof-arounds as well as to the competitive types. And even in the recreational league we're in, the time commitment can seem onerous at times, with two different practice times in the week, and two games per weekend. Add in a weekly piano lesson and a religious-ed class, and we have a solid three school afternoons a week that are spoken for, leaving less time for "regular" stuff like homework, preparing dinner, and just hanging around.

> If you catch yourself thinking that you have to jam more stuff into an already overtaxed schedule so your child doesn't fall behind, stop yourself. There's simply no such thing as "falling behind."

I've very deliberately kept activities to this minimum for a few reasons, chief among them finances and sanity, both of which are limited! But these days, The Parenting Pack can be fairly strident, depending on where you live, in its collective belief that you *should* sign your kids up for what you *can* sign them up for. I've had other parents ask me if I've tried baseball yet (nope) and then tell me, trying to be "helpful," that at my sons' ages, it might be too late. Sadly, that's kind of true; if you don't start with T-ball at age four, you're like the aspiring Olympic gymnast who hasn't been swinging from the uneven bars since she was six. It's too late. There's too much to do!

And if you catch yourself thinking that you have to jam more stuff into an already overtaxed schedule so your child doesn't fall behind, stop yourself. There's simply no such thing as "falling behind." There's a whole world of activities out there, and no one but you should decide—for the health of your child, your family, and your budget—which ones you "need" to do, and when.

Why "The Parenting Pack" is so seductive

Following the crowd has always been tempting. Think back to junior high; it always did seem that if only you had the right jeans or hairstyle, *everything would be so much easier.* But just as it was back then, the seduction was all, and if you managed to get the jeans (against your mother's wishes probably), or had a miracle day on which your hair actually behaved like the cool girls' did, you were still the same person. Hair wasn't happiness.

You know that now, of course, but still following the Pack carries the pull of a siren's song, because it seems right to do things *how they're done.* But it's also insidious, because it discounts your own instinct. The Parenting Pack (and in this group

I include the "experts") seem to have all the answers, except of course, when they don't (TV okay in moderation; TV bad, bad, bad all the time; rice cereal first, rice cereal never), sometimes a 180-degree, whiplash-inducing turn. How can you keep track? You can't, and you shouldn't. Back in my mom's day, you had your own mother's advice to accept, adapt, or reject; ditto for the family doctor or pediatrician. And that was it—and really, wasn't that enough? These days, you have way more than that, a whole chattering cacophony of conflicting, contrasting, fickle advice telling you What Is Right and What Is Deeply, Deeply Wrong.

When you're swayed by the pack mentality so popular these days, you can easily end up miserable without knowing why. I know I've seen it—the moms hanging around at the YMCA while their kids take that one lesson or sport too many, and they're *miserable* about it. Or, okay, maybe not out-and-out miserable, but these mothers aren't floating through their packed schedules with contentment. Some undoubtedly are there because they enthusiastically and confidently believe that being on the run with their kids in their minivans all day, every day, is what is best. If they're happy, that's great. But if they're not? The miserable ones complaining to each other that they never have a moment to themselves? That they keep missing the sign-up for ballet and when is it that we need to buy tickets for the school play and who is the best piano teacher again and does she come to the house? They seem to be moms who have lost their ability somewhere along the line to access the voice inside that tells them what would really make them more relaxed and happy with what they do with their kids, and instead listened to the pack.

Why rejecting "The Parenting Pack" is better for your kids

Hopefully it's clear now why *not following The Parenting Pack* is better for you and your family as a unit. But why is it better, in the long term, *for your child*? You might believe the answer is complicated, but really, it's simple: If you follow the pack, you end up confused, dizzy, possibly miserable, and potentially cash-poor. Is that a good example? Didn't think so. By contrast, *not* fitting in, marching to your own mom beat, questioning (not necessarily rejecting, but for sure questioning) all those "this is the way we do it" expectations about motherhood these days shows your children that you're not a victim of peer pressure. Can you think of a better example for them? It's all in the process—long, sometimes difficult, but ultimately rewarding—of creating independent grown-ups. (And yes, they *are* going to be grown-ups someday, unbelievable as that might be when you're watching your sons trade poopy-diaper jokes at the dinner table, or when they still request a spoon to eat their peas.)

> Not fitting in, marching to your own mom beat, questioning (not necessarily rejecting, but for sure questioning) all those "this is the way we do it" expectations about motherhood these days shows your children that you're not a victim of peer pressure.

But there's an immediate positive effect for your whole family that comes from you breaking away from the pack, identifying what makes you happy, relaxed, and confident as a mother. And it's like this: "If Momma ain't happy, ain't nobody happy." I could list a half dozen things just in the past six months that I considered doing for or with my kids that might have been fun or instructive or cool, but then rejected them for various reasons: too hard to squeeze into a schedule that needs ample time for just hanging out at home; too expensive; too far away. I don't want to do things that'll make me grumpy (or broke). Because when I'm grumpy (or broke), my sons lose out in the long run.

A mother's unhappiness infects the whole house. Better that your child should see—even before his eyes are coordinated with each other, much less with his brain—that *his happiness flows from you, not the other way around.*

A couple of years ago, I had an illuminating and sort of frightening chat with a mom I got to know when both our kids were in preschool. At the time, my husband was out of work. She, like me, was self-employed, and her husband's business, while stable, had taken a hit, too. Bad times all around—I'd say we both fell into the category of hanging on to our rung on the middle-class ladder with both hands white-knuckled. We spent some time relating stories about squeezed finances and other woes. And *then*, after all that—including confiding that she had paid the preschool tuition with her credit card more than once—she told me how she'd signed up her five-year-old daughter for, wait for it...golf.

Yes, you read that right: prekindergarten golf lessons. This was in addition to religious school, soccer, and dance, not to mention preschool and not to mention paying for a sitter for her two younger children.

What she told me was, "There are so many things they can do—I feel like she should try all of them."

So, this nice, smart, and well-meaning mother was losing sleep over money, and dragging herself and her two other children around town, shortchanging work time, her home, and herself, because golf was *there*. Where was the voice that said, when she heard tell of golf lessons for five-year-olds, "Nah, not for us. Don't have the time, the money, or the need." Or the voice that might have said, "Golf? Hey, that gives me an idea. Her grandparents want to know what to get her for her birthday. Maybe I'll suggest some kiddie golf stuff so we can fool around with it in the backyard."

That voice is lost, to her and to many of us.

Mean Mom, Free Mom

Mom misfits like me—those of us who have to fight the urge to roll our eyes heavenward when asked to "shake our sillies out" at a Mommy and Me, the ones who get eye-rolls themselves when they admit that their living rooms actually *weren't* designed by Toys"R"Us—don't get much play these days. Part of the reason is that we're mothering in a culture that says we're supposed to all like, want, and strive for the same things. Part of it is a devotion to experts, rather than instincts.

My point—and I do have one!—is that being a mom misfit can be a good thing. On the surface, when you're not buying the Dino Racecar Barbie Extravaganza at the toy store (or if you are in fact the sort of mother who gets lost and vaguely dizzy even setting foot in Toys"R"Us); when you're not booking the Chuck E. Cheese's party (because there's not enough Xanax or Purell in the world for that); when you're not having one mind-numbing conversation after another with the class mom-automaton who has nothing much to talk about aside from elementary-school gossip; when you're not driving yourself crazy researching an Ivy League-track preschool; when you're not following the pack...you can seem mean indeed. But the payoff down the line is a happier mother and a more balanced kid.

[5]

Mean Mom Manifesto #5:
Take (or Take Back) Control.

A few years back, when I was casually flipping through TV channels, I came across a show, new at the time, on the TLC network—home of such family "reality" programming as *A Baby Story* (an addiction of mine when pregnant) and *Bringing Home Baby*. I have racked my brain, but I can't recall the name of this particular program, because I only watched it the one time and it was cancelled pretty soon after, far as I know.

The premise of it was that each show would focus in on one family's, or mother's, issue: she would present what was vexing her about child-rearing, and then later, in a local coffee shop, a group of other mothers would talk her through it and present ideas and solutions. There was also some help provided from experts, but they were filmed separately. So, it was kind of a mom-to-mom self-help reality show, I suppose you could say.

The one episode I saw stuck with me—it featured a mom

with three young daughters, and she faced the camera in her home and described how she felt overrun by her girls.

Plaintively, she described how, when she became a mother, she had been determined to always offer her children choices, to let them decide what to do, what to eat, what to wear, when and where to go. All. The. Time. As she explained while her daughters ran riot around her, she herself had not been granted choices like this as a child. She was convinced that giving her girls the benefit of choice on *everything* would leave them more confident and self-assured than she had been.

In a way I sort of wish this program had lasted long enough for me to find a clip on YouTube, if only to convince myself that I actually watched it, that it wasn't a bad dream. I remember a lot of details though. For example, we see this mother trying to get her brood breakfasted on a school morning. All three belly up to the breakfast counter, and she asks them what they want. Bonus points for you if you guess that each girl (and in my memory they ranged in age from four or five to eight or nine) wanted something completely different. So she starts up the three differ-ent breakfasts, and then asks them—I swear, I remember this—*what plates they want their food on.* She holds up a handful of kid-themed paper plates in different colors and styles. And—again, you get bonus points, or maybe you shouldn't since it's kind of a giveaway—the girls end up fighting over the preferred style of plate, of which she naturally only has one.

Any wonder this mom is, as the parlance goes, at her wits' end? The girls then proceed to whine and argue over what they'll wear to school and how their ponytails will be arranged. Okay, maybe not that last thing, but it could have been. And what struck me, hard, was that these girls actually didn't seem to have a lot of self-confidence. Oh, they had a certain *kind* of confidence—they were confident that if they whined and moaned enough, they'd get what they wanted, but they never seemed satisfied with that. They had sassiness—if you define "sassy" as "talking back disrespectfully." They had whining down to an art. And they were undoubtedly selfish. You could argue that even with the atrocious behavior they displayed, their mother's decision to grant them choice in every aspect of daily living did accomplish her goal of boosting their self-esteem, but I'd argue against that.

I'd say that in addition to being self-centered—each daughter was like a tiny island unto herself, and damn the comfort or pleasure of her sisters, not to mention her mother or the family as a whole—they appeared to be very unsure of themselves. They seemed to be confusing *getting what you want* (the last blueberry waffle, the pink Minnie Mouse plate) with *being confident*. Or anyway, their mother did.

It wasn't a very pretty picture of family life. And obviously, this well-meaning mother wasn't happy with what she'd created, though it wasn't until she got a gentle dose of reality from her coffee-shop friends that she began to realize why. At the time, my boys were quite young. It's possible, in fact, that neither of them was even talking—the baby still a baby, the toddler not yet willing to express himself in words. And all I could think was, *This will not happen to me.*

My thought was, *Why did this nice mother confuse wanting to treat her daughters kindly and respectfully (as I gather her own parents probably didn't do with her) with letting her daughters have free rein?* I would not turn myself into a servant/short-order cook/enabler of selfish behavior for the sake of self-esteem, which, it seems to me, can be nurtured in children without parents handing over the keys to the castle.

So right then and there was born **Mean Mom Manifesto #5: Take Control!** I saw then, and still maintain today, that remaining in control—remaining the *adult* in the household—is not the same thing as being autocratic or dictatorial. It is, instead, *authoritative.* What that means: When you are authoritative, you project to your children the comforting sense that there is a responsible person at the wheel, that the parents' job is to take care of things, and it's the child's job to, well, grow up. (By contrast, authoritarian parents are those who still live in a "children should be seen and not heard" world.)

> I would not turn myself into a servant/short-order cook/enabler of selfish behavior for the sake of self-esteem, which, it seems to me, can be nurtured in children without parents handing over the keys to the castle.

Authoritative, in-control parents, I hope you come to agree with me, are the kind who raise the most self-confident, self-assured, and humble (in the right ways) adults. Authoritative, in-control parents do not tend to raise kids who think their happiness hinges on getting the last Minnie Mouse plate.

Who's in Charge Here?

That TV mother (every now and again I wonder how she's doing, with what would be by now three teenage girls!) may have had good intentions—who *doesn't* want her child to feel good about herself?—but clearly she was going about it in a way almost hilariously guaranteed to have the exact opposite effect. Giving one's child every choice possible leaves him not empowered, but confused, angry, and selfish. Not what you want, is it? Me neither.

And there's more to it than that, more to it than guarding against breeding selfish, grabby kids. There's the whole issue of control. As in, *who has it?* Who's got her hands on the steering wheel—you or your kids? Here's a tricky truism about children: they want control, badly. That is, if you listen to what they *say*. But they paradoxically *don't* want control, just as badly, if you listen to what lies between the lines of what they say. That was my impression of that pretty trio of girls: In between their whines and moans, you could hear it: "Please, Mom. Please. Just tell us to wear the raincoats because it's raining today, okay? And when we're complaining that we didn't get the plate we wanted? Recite that old saw from preschool: 'You get what you get and you don't get upset.' Really. We grumble and stomp around when we hear it, but we *love* that."

I'm pretty sure that after I pulled my jaw up off the couch on that day I watched this show, I stuck with it long enough to be sure that the moms in the coffee shop, and the expert talking-head the show pulled in for comment, agreed with my take, and thankfully they did. They were possibly gentler than I might have been, if I were there in that coffee shop, hopped up on a grande latte and a low-fat blueberry muffin. This mother—hopeful, harried, bewildered—heard, from her peers and the expert, that her kids *needed her to be in control.* That there were plenty of ways to give her children the self-esteem boost of making their own choices without turning the whole kit and caboodle over to them and hoping for the best.

Ceding control to the pint-size set did not serve this mom's intended purpose of fostering greater self-esteem—she had been confusing *giving them choices with making them feel good about themselves.* But instead it was making them insecure and anxious. And you can't redo your own childhood by way of your children, who aren't an experiment or a project, but people you have the responsibility to grow into adults: hopefully, adults who don't pout when they don't get the plate they want, or the job they feel they deserve, or the car that's as cool as their neighbors', when they've done nothing whatsoever to deserve the job or the car.

Choices are great, and they do make children feel as though they have some say over the outcome of their day, some agency over their lives, but the choices they make should be simpler ones: *Do you want to wear your red sweater or the pink one?* as opposed to *Do you think you should wear a sweater today, considering it's 30 degrees outside?*

Control Issues

The idea of taking control as a parent sounds wonderful, doesn't it? I mean, who *wouldn't* want children who are both self-confident *and* compliant? But control can also be a slippery thing to hold on to, especially when the benefits seem to be long-term (even though many of them aren't, as you'll see) and the downsides feel so immediate and vexing, such as the arguing, the whining, and the pushback. ("But *she* got the pink plate last time!")

Then again, you don't have to wait all that long for the long-term effects to make themselves felt. Here's the thing about whining and talking back: If you nip it in the bud right away, and if you manage the magic trick of consistency, it gets better pretty fast. Oh, sure, you have to do it over and over again— that's the consistency part of it, so maybe it's more doggedness than finger-snapping magic—but eventually the kids realize they can't fight City Hall (of which you are, of course, mayor).

> A household with young children simply doesn't work smoothly if you adopt a one-person, one-vote system.

I believe this with a strength that borders on evangelism: A household with young children simply doesn't work smoothly if you adopt a one-person, one-vote system. In fact, that kind of democratic home—purely democratic, that is, with every person of every age granted the same level of control, even those who haven't fully mastered their mother tongue—is the recipe for chaos.

Take dinner, for example. If you were to ask my sons on any

given day what should be for dinner, you would get a bunch of answers, but essentially it's the same list: macaroni and cheese, plus pizza and hot dogs and maybe some peas. And chocolate milk. Fortunately, they don't choose (though the above foods do make the rotation often enough, though not in the same meal, and on the plates I set out). I choose. Well, along with their father.

When I was a little girl, I'd ask my mother (in the same way my kids do now), "What's for dinner?" And my mother would sigh and say, "Everything you hate." Sounds mean, doesn't it? It wasn't; at least, I don't think so. It was the frustration evident at the end of the day, is all. And truth be told, though I'll eat just about anything now save raw oysters, sushi, and mushrooms, I was a horribly picky eater as a child, so she was often right and it *was* everything I hated. There's a very long pendulum swing from my mother ("Everything you hate") to some of today's mothers ("Well, what do you want, sweetie? Wendy's out or chicken nuggets at home?").

Say *No* to Sippy Cups!

Full disclosure here: I once had almost an entire kitchen cabinet devoted to sippy cups. I tried them all, in search of the elusive "perfect" one. But why, I thought after I'd finally tossed the last one in the recycle bin, had I become a slave to those horrible little mildew-attracting valves that make it possible for a child to drink while upside down? I wish I hadn't. They're pricey (especially because you keep looking for newer/better ones, or because the old ones get lost, or because the one with Disney princesses can't possibly be used by the kid who wants the Transformers one); they're annoying; they're possibly unsanitary. And to me—in retrospect—they represent this tip of the balance from a time when we got our kids ready for a grown-up world (a world that includes being able to drink out of a cup) to a time when we reorganize our world (and our kitchen cabinets) to be child-friendly in the extreme.

In the manufacturers' quest to market a cup that won't spill while the tot is drinking in the car or on the couch, and in our quest to finally find the ideal sippy cup for our kids, we've all stopped asking this question: how about the kids just, you know, *not drink on the couch or in the car?*

When I was still childless, I was in my sister's basement playing a board game with her then-young kids and my father. The kids were drinking from pouches—you know the kind, with the straw you poke through. And I asked my dad—seriously, this occurred to me all at once, that such things as sippy cups and juice boxes didn't exist when I was a child—*what did we used to do?*

He said, dryly, "You drank out of a regular cup, at the table, like a human."

Out of a cup. At the table. Like a human.

We've moved from a time where kids learned how to navigate the big-people world they'd someday inherit, in which people don't drink from silver pouches of juice unless they're astronauts, to a time when it's perfectly normal—in fact when it seems *imperative*—to change the world into a place kids feel comfy. (Which is why, I theorize, cars have so many cup holders. We got so used to making it easy for our kids to sate their hunger and thirst on the go, we began to feel the need for a spot for our grown-up juice boxes, a.k.a. our Starbucks cups.)

So can you do something for me, if you've still got little ones? Can you teach your kid to drink out of a cup? At the table? Like a human? Thanks.

Why did we lose control?

So how did it get this way? How did we reach a point in which there even *is* a TV show about a parent who has no clue that relinquishing control to children who can't reach the buttons on the microwave yet is not a smart, forward-thinking idea? *How did we get to this place?* There have been a few gradual shifts in parenting over the last generation or two that, taken together, seem to make loosening parental control a good idea (even though, when you examine the resulting entitled and unhappy children it can create, it's not at all a good idea).

The strictness shift

Our parents, many of them anyway, were strict. Us? Not so much. Or to qualify that, more of our parents were probably strict than most of today's parents are willing to be. And not only that, or more important than the actual level of strictness, the very fact that they were strict was seen as *normal*, not *mean*. It wasn't something to hide; it was what it was. A parent was strict, or in control and in charge, because *that was her job*. Many of today's parents, by contrast, seem eager, in this as in many other aspects of parenting, to reject rather than imitate whatever our parents did. To reinvent. To be our children's friends rather than their camp commandants.

But isn't there a middle ground? My parents were strict in that traditional sense: I had a bedtime to adhere to, I had to clean my plate, especially of vegetables and even—blech—of liver and onions on occasion. I had chores. But we also had ice cream in the freezer all summer, and my strict parents took us to Disney World when Disney World was still new. It used to be, as I said, that "strict" was the sort of default, everyday position. What some of us seem to remember, though, is having chafed against the rules. We forget the ice cream (and forget, even though we're parents now, too, that perhaps our folks— gasp!—were doing the best they could) and only remember (or more keenly remember) that it seemed *so unfair* that we had to eat what our mothers cooked, no option for boxed mac-and-cheese instead. Or that we had to stick to one after-school sport in high school because we also had familial obligations, chores, religious commitments. That it wasn't, in short, *all about us*.

What my parents were was *in control*. And as a child, I understood that. Not understood it in its subtleties, but I intuitively got its immutable nature. It was what it was; it would not have occurred to me to suggest I have a different plate than my sister, much less a different dinner, or if it had, I would have known that would never fly, it would never even cause my parents to wrinkle their foreheads in consideration. Which doesn't mean I didn't try to worm my way around their control—that, after all, is the job of young children: they find an envelope, and they push against it. But back then we knew that the rules, whatever they were, and whether we liked them, were not necessarily open to negotiation, at least not the ones that truly mattered.

The collective band of parents made their rules for the home, some looser, some tighter (we could not go to a friend's house without a parent being at home; other kids I knew could, for example), and the collective band of children followed the rules, or bucked the rules, or wiggled their way around them looking for loopholes

> That, after all, is the job of young children: they find an envelope, and they push against it.

(like, you know, lying about whether Mrs. Sullivan was going to be home, not that I have any direct knowledge of anything like that going on, ahem). But they didn't ever wonder if perhaps they could *change* the rules.

Of course, that's presuming we're talking about older kids who have the capacity to attempt a negotiation. ("Bed at 8? How about 9? Can we split the difference and call it 8:30?") But the sense that rules or expectations are open to negotiation starts, these days, with babies. Now, it's not that babies are trying to force a coup. ("See, the thing is, Mom, I think it would be awesome if you let me toddle free in Target. Holding me back in this shopping cart is too restrictive for my growing sense of self. I *need* to explore. Preferably in the toy aisle, thanks.") It's that parents themselves wonder that very sort of thing. *If he's squirming in the shopping cart, should I let him out?* We start to think, *I can't believe my parents had me "make do" with my sister's old bike. How awful was that! I'll never do that.* You get the idea: Whatever we can potentially perceive as a too-strict stance, we are liable to try to reverse in our own homes. *Make them share a room? Make them eat the slimy spinach? Make them clean up after dinner? Not us, not me, no way!*

Here's the thing: I hated the spinach, but I ate it, because I knew that it wasn't negotiable. I *hated* cleaning up after dinner when I was old enough to do so (especially on spare rib night, or any night that involved the dreaded broiler pan, ugh), but I did it. And I've got no problem (a) admitting that it did me good, because I learned to follow rules and respect my parents, as well as, eventually, to like vegetables and to know my way around a broiler pan; and (b) letting my kids know, from before they could even really understand what the heck I was saying, that pretty soon it would be them scraping the dishes, loading the dishwasher, and scrubbing the pots. And now we'd be adding composting the scraps to their workload—ha!

(Kids' and parents') Worlds colliding

For a variety of reasons—many more two-job families, many more of us living in isolated communities with fewer kids out playing unsupervised on the streets or in the parks, many more structured activities like sports that require parental supervision and carpooling—our lives and our children's lives feel far more enmeshed than that of the majority of parents and kids in past generations. Whereas I remember my childhood pursuits, indoors or out, being more or less my domain, these days it's more likely that parents are, say, on the floor playing Candy Land, or sitting on a park bench while their children play on the playground, or race-walking behind their bicycles.

Some of these are welcome changes—it's fun to play games with kids (well, to a point!), and some are necessary; in many of our neighborhoods, it's probably not so safe to let a kid roam on a bike on his own. I did, but then I lived on a dead-end cul-de-sac with sidewalks. But some of this shift, some of the worlds-colliding nature of kids and parents, is less welcome, in my opinion, when it leads to parents hovering too much, leaving kids without a parent-free zone.

Back when I was my sons' ages, I spent most of my free time, well, *free*. Without a single day of summer camp to occupy me, the summer was gone in a finger snap without my having played enough Games of Life, or enough games of cul-de-sac-wide flashlight tag at dusk. There were *woods* to explore (and by "woods," I mean the scrubby stand of trees that cluttered the way-back of our yard and our next-door neighbor's yard). There were endless ways to take our games and play them in ways not listed in the directions, or create elaborate fantasy games based on books or TV shows.

I was in control of my sphere (more or less), and my parents were in charge of theirs. Now, with the spheres overlapping, parents feel (rightly) that the kids have less control, and thus try to give them more choices. It's a backward way of looking at things, once you unpack it and realize what's going on, but it's evident nonetheless. I was "free" to make my own choices with my playtime, knowing that (a) my parents weren't interfering and telling, say, my neighborhood friends what to do, or directing what we did; and that (b) when it was no longer playtime, the rules my parents set, such as coming in when called, or (to go back to meals) eating up my spinach no matter how long it took, were in force.

Blurred lines, collided worlds, overlapping spheres: when Mom and Dad are playing on the floor with their kids even if they'd rather jab the Life game's pink and blue stick figures in their eyes, it's almost as though they know too much about their kids' worlds. These days it's hardly odd to hear two moms discussing exactly how their daughters play with their dolls, or how their sons set up the Hot Wheels cars on the living-room carpet and what the rules of his races are—they know all the details, and they know exactly when they have to get the kids to stop and clean up because it's time for the next structured activity. I set up sprawling Barbie-and-Ken worlds on the lawn with my friend, and my parents and hers were just glad we were happily occupied—what we were actually up to was our business.

Kids as "projects"

The children we have—the humans we create or adopt and then hope to keep alive long enough for them to stand on their own and maybe take care of us someday—are not simply our progeny, but projects. And we're good students: if we have a project, we want to ace it. And don't forget: everyone's watching, grading, and judging.

So that means we need to identify and put in place a *system* for raising them, because we firmly believe we can have a decided, quantifiable effect on them. Part of that is a swing of the pendulum in child psychology beliefs: Whereas my parents figured we were who we were as people (which meant it was their job to instill values and teach discipline and send us to school for everything else), and there was little they could do to change that (it was nature), today, it's much more of a nurture focus, a belief in or devotion to cause and effect.

One example springs immediately to mind and is a major topic of parent-to-parent discussion at school plays and soccer fields around here, and that's the issue of the school-start cutoff date. If your kid falls before but near the date, do you hold him back to game the system? This is something that *never* would have occurred to my parents, assuming they were aware of it. Where it was once just one of the rules—you have to be five years old before December 1 or January 1 or whatever your school district's date is—now it is open for parental push-back.

There's a cause and effect: I can give my little girl a chance to build her social skills with another year of pre-K. I can give my petite child a chance to grow a little (and maybe be the kindergarten's Alpha Girl, rather than the kid who cries every day for a month). I can give my son an opportunity to "catch up" with the more-social, school-ready girls, *and* be the bigger, stronger (and maybe someday sports-scholarship-winning) kid in his high school.

When a child is a project, a similar phenomenon happens as when parent/kid worlds collide: We are so hyperaware of and so in control of every aspect of our child's life that—yes, ironically—we treat them as proto-equals whose opinions we want to solicit, believing that doing so will make them smarter and more capable. When all it does is leave them confused—and sometimes infantilized.

Do over!

Our kids are a chance to press "re-do" on our own childhoods. This is related to, but not the same as, my first point. Even when our parents weren't necessarily strict, they did *something* we can't put our fingers on but that we want to change, and since we can't actually go back and re-do our own childhoods, we turn around and try to re-create it, but so much better, with our kids. We will not *look different* from the other mothers. We will not *have different rules* than our kids' friends' parents. If other people have snacks, we'll have snacks. Are you seeing my point here? Our parents seemed unafraid to just...do what they felt was right, and who cared what anyone else did.

When I was a little girl, my best friend Patti lived next door and was two years younger than I was. She was my constant companion from the time we moved in to our house when I was nearly five and she was not yet three. I met her when my mom sent me to her backyard on our first day in the new house. (My older sister had gone to her new school, my dad had gone to work, and I was probably getting underfoot.) There were no fences between the houses in our development as yet, so when my mother saw a little girl digging in a sandbox in the adjacent yard, she just sort of shooed me over there. No introduction, no ringing the other mom's doorbell. Anyway, Patti. When we got a bit older, we'd play for hours in the wooden playhouse in her yard and would come in to our respective homes to ask for picnic lunches. Smart girls that we were, we went to my house for sandwiches, hers for drinks and snacks. We'd get the same sandwiches (peanut butter, bologna, cheese) from either mom, so that wasn't the problem. But if we wanted Strawberry Quik and Ding Dongs? Yeah, that would be from Patti's mother.

It *never once occurred to me* to ask my mother to actually *buy* Strawberry Quik or Ding Dongs, which she wouldn't have anyway (my mom was the Fruit Lady), but if that were today? The mother of the character played by little-girl-me might think, "*My* mother never bought Ding Dongs and it made me sad." Or, "I want *my* house to be known as the place where you can mainline Strawberry Quik."

The impulse to use your parents' example as you work out your parenting style is, of course, inevitable. But when you're looking to redress what you perceive as the "wrongs" or "injustices" of your childhood, you may end up fixating too intently on what was truly unjust or legitimately made you sad: that your father's head was always behind the newspaper when he got home from work; that your mother never signed you up for ballet lessons. If you focus on certain negatives, you may forget the good parts, such as that your dad, though he may have been preoccupied during the work-week, made a point of taking you along on his Saturday errands. You may dismiss what might have not necessarily been their fault, such as that ballet lessons weren't as ubiquitous as they are today. If you are determined to redress wrongs, what may also happen is that you do things as a parent that you wouldn't otherwise have done, things in conflict with your values or that make you feel comfortable. You may start parenting the way other people do because you think that *must* be right, because it makes your child happy for five minutes.

And one of those things might be giving over decision-making control to your child.

It's a kids' world after all

Our world is set up for kids, not (so much) for adults. When I was in junior high, I started watching soap operas after school, and one perennial aspect of this now-dying art form is the way children are handled—which is to say, not much at all. Pregnancies present useful story lines (is it Brock's baby—or his father's?!), as do infants and toddlers (think custody battles). But children can't do much, so they get shunted offset until they're old enough to come back and challenge Brock's father for the family business.

Meanwhile, you don't see much evidence that any of the soap

families' homes *have* children in them. There are no toys on set, no messes, no chicken nuggets on the dining-room table or mud-caked soccer cleats cluttering the foyer. Homes appear utterly untouched and unchanged by the fact that a child lives there.

Our current world is the polar opposite of the average soap-opera set. We live in a world where even a modest living room, when a baby's brought into it, looks like it was staged by the *One Step Ahead* catalog. Or like a day care, or a Little Tikes showroom.

The world is just plain old more set up to emphasize kids' stuff, their comfort, their food needs, their safety, and so on. Don't get me wrong; much as I'd love, in theory, to have a home always humming with order and cleanliness, like a TV show's set, I know that's not possible or desirable. I *do* have kids and they *do* live here, and there *are* small cars so well-camouflaged by our living room rug that I often don't see them and end up cursing and hopping around in pain with a tiny, made-in-China Ferrari stuck to the bottom of my heel. But neither do I desire to have every corner of my domicile look like I'm the stranger here. When we brought our firstborn home, our previously off-white couch gradually turned an off-off-white; let's call it Spit Up Chic. I was okay with that—I knew that maintaining a stain-free couch was as much a fantasy as maintaining my bust's...let's call it perkiness. But that doesn't mean I wanted to cede control to a child who can't keep his food down on a consistent basis.

Whereas parents once brought home children and gradu-ally incorporated them and their stuff—their toys, their shoes, their books, their bikes—into their homes, these days it's more likely, more acceptable (even, often, applauded) for parents to transform their homes before the baby even gets there, and if not, soon after. Hence you see families on shows like HGTV's *House Hunters* "needing" to ditch their 1,800-square-foot home for something *much larger* and *more baby-friendly* because they're pregnant. "Oh, we can't have those stairs; what about little Elijah?" (Um, won't Elijah eventually master the stairs?)

When I was pregnant with my first son, my friend Maria, then a new mother herself, stood in my apartment and said, "Pretty soon this will all be full of plastic and primary colors!"

It didn't happen. Oh, sure, we moved the coffee table to one side of the living room when the baby started toddling, in part to keep him from smacking his face on the table's unforgiving edge, in part because the apartment wasn't huge and giving the boy a clear spot to explore and play seemed the right thing to do. But that small accommodation, plus emptying the bottom portions of our bookshelves to stow his toys and books, and tucking his crib and dresser into a corner of the dining room, was the sum total of Making Our Home Child-Friendly.

These days, in our house, the living room may have those aforementioned cars lurking about, and there may be *Highlights* magazines drifting around the kitchen along with my *New Yorkers* and my husband's *Money*, and yes, there's a playroom in the basement painted in colors I wouldn't have chosen for public rooms of the home, but it's remained mostly a grown-up house, a house for my kids to grow into, as opposed to a house we dumbed down for them.

Take It Back!

So, how do we regain the steering wheel and get—and stay— in control? Before you even try, take heart—by which I mean, don't think that it may already be too late. Once your dining room is overrun by Little Tikes climbing toys and your freezer by chicken nuggets, or your TV remote commandeered by small and sticky hands, it may seem impossible to reverse the trend, but it's not.

First, remember, kids are resilient. It's true: They cry like crazy over a scraped knee, and twenty minutes later they're at play again, knee bandaged and dried-up tears staining their cheeks. Two days later, their enviable rapid cell regrowth means there's hardly a mark on them.

Same thing for changing routines. Rough at first, a few tears, a Band-Aid might be needed, but they get over it. Their cells change over, and soon enough they know that—to use an example in my own house—after dinner, the TV is *Mommy's.* Oh, sure, they can ask, and they do. But the answer is no, sorry, honey. But you can watch *House Hunters* with me if you want.

Second, keep the rewards in mind. Imagine—going back to the start of this chapter—that the mother who wanted to grant her kids greater self-esteem did so by taking *back* control, by telling them that they could have one of two things for break- fast, or that *she* would decide what the TV-watching rules of the house were, or that *she* would be the one who mandated coats on cold days and homework before video games. *Every- one* would be happier.

There are two main things you have to deal with to take control:

1. **Get over wanting your kids to be comfortable at all times.** They won't be, and sometimes—gulp!—you'll be the reason. But it's for a good cause. Think my boys are annoyed when computer time is over for the day, or when they can't have a post-dinner treat on the heels of a food-fest at school that day? Yep, they are. If I gave in, they'd be thrilled with me. But when I don't, their annoyance dissipates pretty quickly. They pushed the envelope. That's their job. I held the envelope's seams firm. That's mine. I'm often gobsmacked by how quickly they give up and forget the whole thing; here I am braced to hunker down for a long battle of wills, and in five minutes they've forgotten the ice pop that *they absolutely had to have* and moved on.

2. **Get over wanting your child to be your best friend.** It feels like a nice idea—you and your children best pals—but it almost never is. Having fun, yes. Cuddling and watching movies on TV, yes. Going out and throwing a football or kicking a soccer ball around? Absolutely. Playing a lengthy game of Monopoly Jr.? Well, leaving that for my husband, but sure. That isn't *being friends*, though. Know how I know the difference? If we're tossing a football, we may be having fun, but I'm still the one who has to say stuff like, "Don't throw it into the tomato plants, please." I'm the one who says, "Did we put sunscreen on the back of your neck before we came out

here?" And I'm the one who says, "Okay, it's getting too dark to see and it's time for Mom to make dinner, anyway." Too many parents hold up this lofty, sweet-seeming goal of their kids viewing them as Best Friends, and it stops them from following through on rules and being in control. If you're your child's best friend, you're not holding the envelope firm while your child tries to rip through it. To overuse a metaphor.

Top Five Reasons to Stay on Top

1. **Control over the TV.** *You* get the remote control. *They* have to ask for it. Trust me, this is priceless. Because you took heart and took control, you not only don't have a TV in every room to appease the troops (I realize this is a personal/family decision, but having one TV is working for us so far, with an "extra" set in the basement solely for video games—for a half-hour a day max), but you also don't have to beg and wheedle to get to watch HGTV. They're the ones who should wheedle.

2. **Control over the décor.** Who says Fisher-Price should rule the roost? If you're in charge at home, you aren't stuck with dinner guests who have to sit on a small plastic chair or drink out of a Transformers cup. Because you took heart and took control, you kept the important-to-you adult stuff in place in your house, and, eventually, with

practice and consistency, your kids learned things such as "no grape juice on the dining room chairs."

3. **Control over treats (yes, I said it: I hide ice cream from my kids).** When you decide on simple (but profound!) things like the menu, you can, with the impunity and pride that comes with, you know, *being an adult*, eat the ice cream after the kid goes to bed. Or whatever your poison is. Because you took heart and took control, you don't always feel the guilt that might lead you to say, *I should probably save the mint choc chip for the kids*. But there's no reason you should stock up with bomb pops and not slide a little low-fat, slow-churned whatever-you-like (if that's what you like) in there, too. And if your kids, like mine, say, "Hey, can I have some of this?" the in-control parent can say, "That's grown-up ice cream" and not feel an ounce of guilt (over the kids—the ice cream's another story).

4. **Control over the meaning of "birthday gift."** When you're secure in your adult-centered life, you're not thrown into a twice-yearly tizzy (at the kids' birthdays and during the holiday season) when you realize you never even pulled out last year's toys because the playroom, and the kids' rooms, and the den, and the living room, and liberal portions of the kitchen and bathrooms are already saturated with toys. Because you took heart and

took control, you nixed grandparental-over-generosity, or (if you really couldn't get your parents or in-laws to quit showering your children with the biggest or loudest stuff in Toys"R"Us) you instituted a firm one in, one out rule (and the charities love you for it).

5. **Control over, well, how they turn out.** When you're at the wheel, you're more likely to end up with kids who don't feel as though they're entitled to be the center of any universe. This is the biggie, the kicker, the serious one. If you skimmed this whole chapter up until here, read this part: When parents let the reins go slack (and remember I'm not talking about super-rigidity—if nothing else, parenting has to be fluid and flexible—but about retaining your position as the buck-stops-here person), when they bend rules so far they snap under their own weight, or don't have rules *at all*, they may get the immediate gratification of kids who high-five you for being super cool. But those same kids will also be walking all over you. (And the couch. With muddy sneakers.) And if they walk all over *you*, they'll feel it's possible to walk all over, say, their teachers. Or their bosses. Not pretty.

[6]

Mean Mom Manifesto #6: Say *No*. Smile. Don't Apologize. Repeat as Necessary.

C an we talk about vending machines? In particular, how much I hate them? Well, not hate *them* so much as continually annoyed that they're always conveniently located right where my kids will pass them all the time. Two places in particular: the YMCA gym and the library. Yes, the library. On the one hand, a vending machine can be a terrific amenity, when it's stocked with decent choices for snacks and drinks alongside of or in place of the usual junk. But when it's just sitting there, a hulking, blinking, enticing reminder to children who approach them that *a snack can be theirs—instantly*—well, then it arouses my ire.

Take our library, for example, a place I love so much I'd marry it if I could. Recently built and cleverly designed, its lower level, where the children's department is, may technically be a basement, but it has floor-to-ceiling windows that look out onto a garden that's been carved out of a hill. I mention this because the children's area shares this non-basement basement with an open seating area furnished with tile flooring and metal café tables and chairs. It's meant to be used as a gathering space (and ends up being occupied, most of the time, by students working with tutors, library staff on a break, itinerant laptop users who like this spot better than Starbucks, or the usual smattering of elderly folks and moms and kids waiting for whatever movie, exercise class, or seminar is about to take place in the program room). Naturally it makes logical sense, if you're going to supply machines, to place them here—and I'm quick to point out that there's a coffee machine as well as one that dispenses yogurt, sandwiches, and whole fruit alongside the machines hawking the usual chips, candy, and soda.

But now, because this vending area exists at all, and because it exists in such close proximity to the children's room, my kids have quickly (they're no dummies) associated *going to the library* with *getting a snack*. As in, "Come on, guys, let's go to the library!" is followed quickly with, "Can we get a snack while we're there?!" Never mind that it is, say, 10 a.m. on a Saturday.

Those two phrases—*going to the library* and *getting a snack*—are, it should go without saying, two strings of words that did not often, if ever, meet up in my childhood.

I have explained to my boys, sometimes patiently but more often with growing exasperation, that going to the library is about books (and, these days, DVDs and Wii games, tickets to local museums, Lego Club, and computers), not about another opportunity to shoehorn a snack into the day. But the immutable fact that there are vending machines in the library does not exactly add weight to my argument; quite the opposite, in fact.

It's naturally my own fault that I said *yes* once—habits form quickly when they come sprayed with the crack that is nacho cheese flavor—though I did, and do, try to steer them toward pretzels or popcorn. But—and here's the key part of this vending machine anecdote—my having said *yes* once, or now and then, or even every other time, doesn't preclude me from saying *no* when I mean the answer to be *no*. Such as when it does happen to be 10 a.m., or right before lunch, or when I don't have the change (or pretend I don't have it). I don't particularly enjoy saying *no* (okay, that's a little bit of a lie; in truth I kind of like it, but I'm funny like that), but I have no problem saying it when it's the right thing to say. I'm not afraid to touch *no* with a ten-foot pole.

Too many parents, though, *are* afraid of the big, bad *no*. Or they are seduced by the sweet, sweet power of *yes*. The power to bring that smile, however fleeting, to their child's face. But please, don't be afraid of *no*. It doesn't bite. Oh, it can *have* a bite, but the sting fades much more quickly than you might think. If you give in to *yes* all the time, not only does it inevitably lose

> Too many parents, though, are afraid of the big, bad *no*. Or they are seduced by the sweet, sweet power of *yes*.

its power (what *else* can you give me besides those Doritos, Mom, hmmm?), but it also causes you to forget, assuming you ever truly knew it, that *no* is pretty darn great all by itself.

Which is why I bring you **Mean Mom Manifesto #6: Say
No. Smile. Don't Apologize. Repeat as Necessary.**

No Kidding!

The reason it's not simply "say *no*," or, à la Nancy Reagan's
anti-drug message in the 1980s, "just say no," is that just *no*
isn't powerful enough. It doesn't always work, doesn't always
take. *No* by itself, not always but a lot of the time, practically
invites push-back. *But you promised* (I did no such thing), *but
it's no big deal* (says who?), *but just this once...*(that's how crack
became an epidemic, son). *No* gains its power when you say it
firmly, with a smile (enigmatic and fixed smiles are best, with
eyes focused on the middle distance, I've found), with limited,
straightforward, and easily repeated reasons, but—and this is
key—*without* an apology (except for the firm kind, such as "I'm
sorry, but the answer is *no*, and the next time you ask I'm afraid
it will *still* be *no*").

And then you repeat, as I said, as often as necessary because,
as we all know, children are not the best at taking *no* for an answer,
or taking any answer without lobbing back another question.

This happens to me, unfortunately, with the library vending
machine so often that I have had to preempt the entire discussion by saying either, "Come on, guys, get your shoes on; we're
going to the library. *If* you're good, we *may* get a snack on the
way out because it *might* happen to also be snack time," or
"Come on, guys, get your shoes on; we're going to the library

and *don't even ask me about the snacks because we're not getting one this time."*

I've also fought the battle of the vending machine at our local YMCA, where for a while last winter my sons were enrolled in a sports-skills class that took place in the immediate pre-dinner hour. I'd sit and wait for them in a chair in the hall outside the gym, right next to a vending machine. When the kids filed outside a few times each hour-long class to grab a drink from the water fountain, *every single kid* who also had a parent hanging around waiting would ask or beg for a treat—or simply assume one would be forthcoming. I stood my ground. It was hard, but I did it. On the last day, they got what they had wanted the whole session: a $1 bag of cookies that they split after dinner that night. And you know what? It's true what they say: The well-earned, longed-for treat is all the sweeter. My *yes* felt sweet, their enjoyment of my *yes* felt sweet—and I know the cookies were sweet because I snagged one for myself.

Why Have We Gotten So High on *Yes*?

Is it too simple to say that *yes* feels good and *no* feels oogy? Sometimes the simplest explanations fit the best. Take that vending machine again; if you're faced with a hopeful (but *this close* to whining) kid, plus a machine full of treats, plus the fact that any one of those treats is, what, $1, give or take? You start to calculate, and begin to think that a $1 *yes* will buy you peace and happiness. Whereas you can keep the dollar and get the whining.

What that calculation fails to add in is the long-term effect of the *yes*. It may feel good right now, but then you've created an expectation that isn't going to stop. And my apologies if this is starting to feel like one of those "what time will the train get to the station" word problems from the sixth grade!

Leaving aside math, and vending machines, let's dig into why *yes* is so much more in favor now than *no*.

We live in a *yes*-happy time

Yes falls neatly into place in our current culture's slavish devotion to easy gratification. You need information? *Yes*, your touchscreen phone will get you the "who was that actor in that movie" tidbit in seconds. You want to watch your favorite movie, or a TV show you missed? *Yes*, you can stream that live, right now. You want to go shopping? Chances are the mall is open, or at least jcrew.com is. You hungry? *Yes*, you can have a snack! And it's not just kids. Back in the day, the very idea of eating on the run seemed...odd somehow, or something one did in an emergency. You wouldn't think of eating on the train, for example; you'd eat at home and *then* get on the train. Neither would you snack while shopping, drink coffee while driving if you weren't a long-distance trucker, or treat every meeting or get-together as a reasonable time to eat. But now we eat everywhere, all the time, and no one looks twice.

The instant-everything culture isn't *all* bad. I do like being able to answer trivia questions with a quick stop at Google. I like being able to food shop on Sundays (whereas grocery stores once weren't even open on this supposed "rest" day). But it's had an effect on kids: waiting has evolved into a quaint, odd concept; something that used to be built into life is now something parents have to *teach*, or even artificially construct. But not all parents do it. We are so caught up in this *right here, right now* moment that it can end up feeling somehow wrong or mean or unnecessarily stubborn of us, as parents, to say *no*, or its corollary, *not right now*. Right now is what it's all about in our culture.

Nice-guy syndrome

Well, maybe "nice mom" syndrome is more apt. Saying *yes* is an ego boost. For you. When you're the mom who says *yes* to the request for a lollipop being offered to the child by the bank teller (even though it's twenty minutes to lunchtime), you're the mom who gets treated to the beaming smile (from the sugar-happy kid as well as from the teller). When you're the mom who says *yes* to the $45 sandals the tween *has to have right now or she'll just die*, you get a contact high off her happiness. And moms of tweens know that those "you're the best mom ever!" moments are fleeting and mercurial at best, and so perhaps can't be blamed for giving in to the urge to grab it while they can.

> We are so caught up in this *right here, right now* moment, that it can end up feeling somehow wrong or mean or unnecessarily stubborn of us, as parents, to say *no*, or its corollary, *not right now*.

But those *yes* boosts are like a sugar high, and it's not just because of the lollipop. You feel good, really good, when you get to say *yes* to your child. You feel so nice. You pat yourself on the virtual back: "I'm the fun one! I make my child happy!" But let me be the sourpuss who asks the questions: Does it last? Or is there another request right behind it? Listen, I'm just like any other mother in that I want that feeling; I crave it. We all do. But the lollipop example? I have to say *no* to that sometimes because have you looked around? There are lollipops (or their equivalent) everywhere, and you can't have every lollipop that's offered or your tongue would be permanently food-dyed some hideous unnatural color (and you'd never eat your lunch).

Yes may be quick, expedient, and an ego boost, but *no* or *maybe later* is only a teeny temporary disappointment. Here's the key: You delay your child's gratification by saying *no* or *maybe later*, but you also delay your own ego boost. And frankly, I'd rather forgo the instant boost of *yes* and wait for the longer-lasting ego gratification of raising a smart, self-confident child who actually *can* delay gratification (or, you know, save up her own money for the $45 sandals or shop wisely for a less pricey version).

No is so last generation!

Yes is (or might be) the antidote to all the *no* you heard growing up. We've been here before, but it bears repeating. If you had *no* parents, whether it was because it was more the done thing back when you were a kid (fewer lollipops, real or metaphorical, out in the world), or because they didn't have the means to give you everything you asked for, or even if it was because there was less to *have* then (it's easy to say *no* when there isn't a drive-through attached to every restaurant, and when every store isn't open all the time), you may be inclined to reverse the trend for your own kids. You may believe that doing so will bond you and your child more tightly, that it will make the two of you—wait for it—friends. But be careful what you wish for. A child who is made to believe the answer will always be *yes* (to the vending machine treat, the pricey shoes, the too-late-for-her-own-good bedtime) never learns where the edge of the envelope actually is. Just wait until her college professor, or her first boss, tells her *no*.

Yes is cooler than *no*

Yes makes you look like one of the "in" crowd of moms. I admit it freely: It's tiring to be the *no* mom, believe me, and not just because—think about it—you only have to say *yes* one time to any given request, but if you say *no* you have to say it a *lot*. Tiring.

During the eight weeks or so of that YMCA class I mentioned earlier, when I said *no* to opening my wallet and dispensing those magic dollars the kids think exist solely for vending machine use, I had to brace myself each time for the push-back. I had to make the mental decision that my *no* would stay firm each time. I had to distract and divert and get them to put on their jackets and walk past the machine each and every time. It never actually felt good, at least not in the moment, and when you're flat-out exhausted in the moment, it's hard to remember how it will feel good *later* that you staved off another opportunity for the quick-fix treat. Two boys facing a tempting glass-windowed display of neatly stacked treats—Chips! Orange things! Gummy worms!—can be persuasive, or maybe relentless is a better descriptor. Handing them the dollars would make me look like the other moms around me who barely registered the "Mom, can I get..." before they handed over the cash.

But I didn't *want* to look like those moms because when you look a little closer? They don't look cool or carefree, dancing through the halls of the Y sprinkling dollar bills out of their own magic wallets while rainbows arch around them and unicorns dance among the Cheetos. It's not that they were the breezy happy moms and I was the dour mean one. In fact, they looked annoyed and harried, not like moms bestowing such benevolence that their grateful kids would give them a kiss on the cheek. So what did they gain? One, a kid who probably was not going to eat dinner without a battle, which is bad enough. But also a kid who would from then on see any vending machine not as a possible, hopeful, maybe-we'll-get-it-this-time option, but a *right he deserves*. Not cool. And also, when you think about it, in the long run, a lot more tiring.

Yes makes memories

This one may be most insidious, because really, who doesn't want to be the parent who creates a childhood full of sweet memories? But be careful if every time you're faced with a yes-or-no situation, you lean toward *yes* purely because you believe it'll create some ideal, preservable memory for your child.

In fact, I believe that fewer, more carefully considered *yeses* create a nicer stream of pleasant childhood memories than endless, indiscriminate ones. They won't remember every single time you said *yes* to the ice-cream vendor or the trip to one of those cheesy amusement fairs that end up costing an arm and a leg (and a bit of vomit sometimes, sorry). But they will remember the time you stopped at that intriguing looking homemade ice-cream place by the side of the country road. You weren't going to stop, but they asked, and it seemed like a really good time to toss out a *yes*. They will not forget it—because *that's* where the memories happen.

· *Yes* and *No* at a Glance ·

Kids ask for everything. This should not surprise anyone who's been a parent for more than three-and-a-half minutes. But sometimes, in the moment, it's hard to see what could be so *wrong* with saying *yes* to things that you've previously said *no* to. There are, it turns out, both immediate and longer-term ills. I'm not saying these are hard and fast rules, but I am saying, buyer beware. Go ahead and say *yes* to the toy at Target, for example, even if you told them *in the car* that there would be no extra toys that day, if you care to deal with the blowback. And it'll come, the blowback. Check this chart to see what I mean:

WHAT THEY'RE ASKING FOR:	WHEN YOU SAY *YES*, YOU MAY GET...	WHEN YOU SAY *NO*, YOU MAY GET...
Candy before dinner	**Now:** a few minutes' peace, maybe a smile from the kid with the blue-tinted teeth. **Later:** a kid who pushes away dinner, and anyway, he didn't even say thank you (that is, easy come, easy forgotten)	**Now:** grumbling, foot stomping, "you're mean," "why not?" "what's the big deal?" **Later:** kids who eat their dinner, more or less, and kids you feel deserve a treat some other, surprise time.

WHAT THEY'RE ASKING FOR:	WHEN YOU SAY *YES*, YOU MAY GET...	WHEN YOU SAY *NO*, YOU MAY GET...
A toy at Target	**Now:** a few minutes' peace (sense a pattern yet?), a smile, but possibly not a thank you (after all, why thank the earth for giving you, you know, *air*?). **Later:** a slimmer wallet, another broken toy kicking around under the couch.	**Now:** whining, but you're a big girl; you can confidently ignore it while steering your cart to the 75% off rack in Women's. **Later:** complete forgetfulness of the once-desperately-longed-for item. Gets easier the next time, and the next.
Money for an online "club"	**Now:** a whoop of joy as you hear your credit-card number being typed into Club Penguin. **Later:** well, you probably know.	**Now:** blah blah blah "you're so mean" blah blah blah. **Later:** a gradual disinclination to buy snuffies or scruffies or whatever they're called, and a search for free online games or ways to look at their friends' houses via Google Earth.
More time for a video game	**Now:** quiet, depending on whether you were smart enough to set up the game system in the farthest reaches of the basement. **Later:** glazed eyes and far too much devotion to Mario or Wii Sports Boxing replays in the kitchen.	**Now:** major, *major* pushback, if you have the kind of kid drawn to games like moths to flame (or my son to dessert). **Later:** kids without the telltale, "I spend all my time in the basement" pallor.

WHAT THEY'RE ASKING FOR:	WHEN YOU SAY *YES*, YOU MAY GET...	WHEN YOU SAY *NO*, YOU MAY GET...
A TV show you don't like	**Now:** insta-Mom-cool street cred. **Later:** bad language at the table.	**Now:** a long and furious discourse on why the other shows are "for babies" (and a refusal to listen to the reasonable suggestion that there are other things to do besides TV, for babies or not). **Later:** grumbles die down and—surprise!—kid finds that there indeed *are* other pursuits to, well, pursue.
Brand-name pricey footwear	**Now:** see above on the street cred, which you may get as it brushes off your super cool, well-shod child. **Later:** another trip to buy more shoes when he grows out of these in eight months.	**Now:** dramatic exhortations about how lame you are (and how lame he'll look). **Later:** the potential to have a discussion about earning and saving money to fill the gap between what you'll spend for shoes he'll grow out of in eight months, and what the pricey stuff costs.

WHAT THEY'RE ASKING FOR:	WHEN YOU SAY *YES*, YOU MAY GET...	WHEN YOU SAY *NO*, YOU MAY GET...
To see an R-rated movie (or PG-13 for the younger-kid set)	**Now:** more cool factor (really, people, you *can't* re-do high school), plus you get to feel cooler than that other dour mother who said *no*. **Later:** the younger kid asking you, "Why did Charlie call me a 'douche bag'?"	**Now:** a majorly embarrassed tween who has to tell her friend that *her* mom is *so mean*. **Later:** the opportunity to talk about the meaning of the word "appropriate" (and, if it was a horror movie she wanted to see, the chance to tell her about the time you slept on your sister's floor for a full week after she saw *Damien: Omen II*).
A "different" dinner than what you've prepared	**Now:** surefire clean plate. **Later:** more dishes to wash. And a guarantee that you'll be making Kraft Macaroni and Cheese (instead of actually eating *your* dinner) tomorrow, too.	**Now:** hearing all about how he'll surely starve to death. **Later:** a child who—surprise!— didn't starve after all.

What's So Fabulous About *No*?

If I've convinced you that *yes* is ephemeral, fleeting, sugary-sweet, and to be reserved for special occasions, I'm pleased. But that's still only half the equation. If *yes* is to be used as sparingly as the fats at the tip of the food-guide pyramid, then let's travel on down to the bottom of the pyramid to the fruits-and-veggies. Let's talk about *no*. *No* may not give your kid the rush of opening a new toy or the weird-colored tongue of the barbershop lollipop, but it offers a lot else. It takes nerve and an extra helping of guts sometimes, but *no* wields great power, and great, long-term, slow-dissolving, fill-you-up satisfaction when properly used. Here's what I mean:

No is power

I know what you're likely to think, as you're reading the phrase "*no* is power." I don't mean power in the absolute or rigid, autocratic sense, but in the buck-stops-here sense. Please don't tell my sons this, but *of course* they have power over me, great power, that rests in their gorgeous faces, their big, hazel eyes, the way they genetically express their father and me and everyone who came before them. They're my *children*, and they can wrap me around their little fingers, as any child worth his salt should be able to do (otherwise no squalling newborn would ever be fed on such a demanding basis, really). But I've got one thing I can hold onto: I've got *no* in my arsenal. *Can we play Wii after dinner?* "No, sweetie, you know that we don't have screen time then. But you can practice piano or play Uno. With Dad." *Can we order pizza for dinner?* "No, guys, it's Wednesday. Friday is pizza day; you know that." *No* gives me that buck-stops-here power that, frankly, I need (unless I want to go broke and get fat eating pizza or hot dogs seven days a week).

No is a teachable moment

I cringe, often literally, when I hear or use the phrase "teachable moment" because it's kinda smarmy, but there are times it's useful. Every time you say *no* and there's a darned good reason for it, you've got a neatly packaged opportunity to get a point across, or to hammer home a point you've already made in four hundred other ways (again, parenting is nothing if not repetitive). Like this: When you say, "No, honey, we can't get the Magic Moon Glow-in-the-Dark Worms you saw on TV, and here's why." (Pick your reason: we don't do worms, period; "magic" isn't what you think it is—let me tell you a story about seahorses ordered through a magazine ad in 1974; I don't happen to think that's the best use of $19.95 plus shipping and handling; and so on). The teachable-moment type of *no* is a way to share values, as well as to explain things like how TV ads are specifically designed to make you believe you *need* Magic Moon Glow-in-the-Dark Worms, but guess what, honey? *You* get to decide what you really, truly want and need.

Additionally, when you say *no* to a birthday party invite because it conflicts with a soccer game and you are already missing another soccer game—which I just did, by the way— you get to teach them that choices have to be made, that you can't do everything that's in front of you, and that when you do something like joining a team (soccer), it's important to show up for as many games as possible because your teammates depend on you. When you say *no* to the truly nasty candy (let's use Fun Dip as a ready example, a bunch of which I just fished out of a party goody bag and tossed), you get to explain how some candy sometimes is a good thing, but there are kinds of candy that are not worth it. I'll always say *no*, for example, to bright-blue cotton candy, after the one time I said *yes*, at a recent minor-league baseball game. It turned their whole faces, teeth and gums included, a Smurf-like ghostly blue. For *days*. (Actually, I don't have to say *no* to that—they quickly announced that they wouldn't have it again, and next time would ask for ice cream. Victory!)

No builds character

Let me put this as simply as possible: Kids who hear *yes* all the time believe that they deserve to hear *yes* all the time. Those are the kids who end up shocked—shocked!—when they are expected to pay their dues in a low-rung job for a while after college. Those are the kids who think every good report card—heck, even every mediocre report card—is cause for a few bucks (or a new pair of boots) to be thrown their way. They're the kids who think stickers on charts that build up to new Matchbox cars, Barbie dolls, or WWE action figures are their birthright. If a *yes* often amounts to empty calories, a *no* is the opportunity to consume a bowl of whole-grain cereal with fiber-rich strawberries and milk for breakfast; it sticks to the ribs.

> Kids who hear *yes* all the time believe that they deserve to hear *yes* all the time.

No makes an eventual *yes* so much better

I mentioned the part where my boys got the measly $1 bag of cookies from the YMCA vending machine, right? I bet those tasted awfully good. This makes logical sense—I'm sure many parents, even those who tend to be serial *yes*-ers, understand this intellectually. I'm sure most of us understand that a constant stream of *yeses* can make kids squishy, entitled, unaware that there's a number of ice cream sundaes or trips to Disney that are too many, because don't they get to have it all? We *understand* it, but we don't always follow through. (I, in part, blame that little kids have eyes that are too large for their faces. When they're just asking, not whining, they look just too darned cute, like puppies, and I'm not even a dog person.)

But we get ourselves into some potentially bad trouble when we overuse *yes* and underuse *no*. Because it's the very thing we hope to achieve with the *yes*—pleasing our child, making him happy, giving him something he wants or that we want for him for whatever reason—that we ultimately undermine with all the *yeses*. The joy decreases as the number of *yeses* rises, because the sense that *the* yes *is most certainly coming* spoils the impact of it.

No promotes a critical, thoughtful mind (yours and your child's)

Wait, what did I just say—what's that mumbo jumbo about a critical mind? Aren't we talking about whether the kid can have another *Cars* car or a pair of Ugg boots? What does saying *no*—and standing firm on the *no*, whatever your reasons for taking that stance—have to do with developing critical thinking skills? Plenty, and allow me to explain. My kids, like all red-blooded Americans, see things they want—on TV, in stores, at their friends' homes. If the answer to everything they saw and wanted was *yes*, we'd all miss the chance to say, "No, and here's why."

The "here's why" is the key here, and it can start from very, very young. *Here's why* you can't have that toy car, honey: That's not why we're in the toy store today. You have a hundred of those cars. This is just an example, but there's more. *Here's why* we can't go to Disney this year: We can't afford it right now. We all love it, don't we? We had such a good time there. And it'll be so much fun when we get to go there again. *Here's why* you may not want that [cheap piece of crap, take your pick] you see on TV: TV commercials are designed to show even the silliest, most useless, poorly made item as though it were something you just *have* to have (see: Magic Moon Glow-in-the-Dark Worms, which aren't real but are close to what actually *is* offered on TV).

But we can say *no*, then look at it and see *why*. That's critical thinking. You're doing it yourself by saying *no*, and you're teaching it by example when you say *no*.

Don't Apologize!

Yes is such a seductive word, especially when you say it to your children. *Yes* is so pretty you want to touch it all the time. It's sweet, like a tray of those fancy-pants cupcakes that are so popular these days, with mile-high tooth-achingly sweet icing. But using *yes* too liberally is the equivalent of eating that whole tray—you get the sugar rush, but then the stomachache, the crash, the regret. *No*, on the other hand—oh, lovely *no*—is powerful. Think of it as handsome rather than fluffy-pretty. A sensible slice of carrot cake, say, or *one* yummy cupcake enjoyed immensely with no ill aftereffects.

No is delayed gratification. *No* builds character. *No* gives moms and dads some private time or a bit of mind-recharging space before launching into another game of Trouble just now.

But what's even better than a well-placed *no* now (to the board game, the Hershey's Kiss, the extra twenty minutes at the playground when you really need to leave right now)? What's even better is a *no* that's *not prefaced by, or followed up with, an apology.*

Ah yes, the no-apologies thing. Even if *no* makes you feel mean, even if it sometimes makes you feel squeamish (*Am I doing the right thing? What harm would it really do if I said yes even though I told them no already?*), it shouldn't! Not

> Saying you're sorry for saying *no* only undercuts your stance—not to mention your authority.

just because you're right to say *no* when it's warranted, but because the *no* is nothing to be sorry for. In fact, saying you're sorry for saying *no* only undercuts your stance—not to mention your authority.

Let me back up a bit. *Of course* you should apologize if you do something bad (you let the f-bomb slip during breakfast, not that I have any direct experience with that, *cough, cough*; or you gossip nastily about a neighbor in their presence; or you yell in that screaming-banshee way of yours, out of proportion to their misbehavior—again, not something I, uh, have direct experience with but I've heard about, ahem). Of course you should apologize, own your own bad behavior.

But if you say *no* to a treat or a trip or a purchase or staying longer when it's time to go? Well, no apologies necessary, because you're the Decider, to borrow a phrase from some guy who used to be our president.

Also—and this is important—because there are *apologies* and then there are *abject apologies*. I'm in favor of the former and way against the latter. Here's the difference:

+ **Apology:** *No, honey, I know you feel sad about this, and I'm sorry about that, but we have to pack up our stuff and leave now because Mommy has to get to work.* This? This is calm, clear, authoritative without being unkind, and it has the wonderful bonus of acknowledging your child's feelings. (*Sucks, hon, but there it is: we have to go.*)

+ **Abject Apology:** *Oh, my poor sweeties. I know, it's awful that we can't go on vacation this summer to that supercool place your friend went to. It's awful for all of us! We are so, so, so sorry it's a no this year."* This one? Hmmm... can you say *victim mentality?* That's akin to saying, "You deserve a trip like your friend had, and your dad and I suck for being so profligate with our money—the mortgage! food! silly us!—that we can't afford it. You. Poor.

Thing." There you go: do that often enough, and you'll have an entitled professional victim on your hands. Hint: that does not look good on a college application or a résumé.

No: What's in It for You?

I've found—and I hope you do, too—that *no* is very freeing for me. I know I'm going to say *no* to certain things (dessert before dinner, or *SpongeBob* after dinner) because those are just rules. That fact, however, never stops my kids from asking, and pushing, and whining. But if I know (firmly and kind of smugly, if I'm being honest) in my own head that the answer will be and will continue to be *no*? *I'm free. Free of the fingernail-chewing possibility of rethinking or engaging in negotiation.* Try it. Practice your enigmatic *no* smile in the mirror. Trust me. It's awesome.

[7]

Mean Mom Manifesto #7:
Teach Life Skills. If Not You, Who?

I very rarely wash my car—embarrassing to admit, but there you go. It's not that I don't know how, I'm quick to point out (in fact, as kids we washed the family cars all the time, and I liked it, liked knowing how to do it, how to soap up and polish and shine the family wagon). But now, with all the rest I have on my plate, it's just one of those things that consistently slips to the bottom of my to-do list, and so I drive around with a film of dirt on the outside and drifts of sand and debris on the inside. At least I can give myself a pat on the back for outlawing (most) kid-eating in the car, so I don't have piled-up empty juice boxes and Goldfish crumbs moldering on the floor. And also in my own dirty-car defense—and, Mom, I'm speaking to you here—isn't it more important to have clean toilets than a clean Toyota? I mean, if we're weighing priorities.

The reason I mention this is that whenever I have a chance to get the car washed by a group of students holding a car-wash fund-raiser, I jump at it. It warms my sentimental heart to know that school clubs and sports teams still use the humble car wash as a means of raising cash, just as I used to do in high school, back when we had to haul the water from the local stream (kidding). And it warms my frugal heart to only spend $5 or $10, rather than the high price the professional car washes charge. (Okay, the kids don't vacuum the inside, but I can get around to that eventually).

Recently, a car-wash fund-raiser had been set up in the parking lot of a local elementary school on an autumn Saturday, when the lot was packed with cars coming and going for kids' soccer games. "Aha!" I thought. "A clean car awaits!" and after one of my kids' games, I steered my poor crusty Toyota over to give it a bath. This time the high-school cheerleading squad happened to be the ones wielding hoses and sponges and wrung-out beach towels. And although they were doing brisk business, I have to tell you, these young women had *no idea* how to wash a car. I mean, they had *some* idea, but it was very rudimentary, involving getting the car mostly wet and sort of soapy, then rinsing and then...well, the drying off thing seemed to elude their understanding.

One girl carried the sponge in her hand as though it was some kind of slime-laden alien life-form. These girls could make pyramids out of their bodies and do splits, but efficiently use towels? Not so much. At one point, and I swear I am not making this up, one cheerleader was walking toward my finally-sort-of-clean-and-rinsed car with a towel draped over her comely shoulder when the cell phone tucked in the waistband of her shorts must have beeped. She stopped a foot from my car, pulled out the phone, and proceeded to text someone back while standing outside my window, oblivious to the wet car, not to mention to the puzzled and increasingly annoyed driver waiting with a $5 bill in her hand and a hungry soccer player in the backseat.

My mind? Boggled. But also intrigued. And in case you think I have a grudge against cheerleaders—either because their predecessors didn't choose me for the squad when I tried out freshman year in a fit of wanting-to-be-cool, or because I miss my seventeen-year-old legs, which I do, but that's another story— it's not just them I'm calling out. In fact, I'm sure the Booster Club and the wrestling team and the Spanish Honor Society aren't champion car-washers, either (I've seen 'em).

Okay, so no one ever taught these young women (or the Honor Society kids or the Booster Clubbers) how to wash a car. Should they know how? I'm thinking yes. Maybe not specifically that skill, but if you use "know how to wash a car" as a metaphor for other useful, if sometimes slightly anachronistic, life skills, then I think not knowing is a bad thing generally.

I tried to be generous, sort of, while thinking about my car-wash cheerleader: maybe she baby-sits her four little brothers after school, so it's only fair her dad do the car washing and the lawn mowing and the leaf raking and snow shoveling (assuming her father even *does* those chores himself, given that all of them are relatively cheap to outsource). Maybe a mountain of school-work and hours of cheering practice and competitions jam-pack her schedule, and her parents are loath to pile anything else on.

But it's not just about the time, because remember I'm using the car-washing skill as a metaphor for other life skills and chores that my generation was routinely taught—and expected to do. I'm thinking that this sixteen- or seventeen-year-old had been, like many girls and boys her age, sheltered and shielded from learning how to do stuff like this in the belief that it's just not necessary anymore. And also, that there's something vaguely *icky* about it—why should she wash a car, except as a fund-raiser for her team, when she could/should be doing other things, like studying for the SAT?

But it *is*. Necessary, I mean, not icky. Thing is, it's not just knowing how to do any specific chore or skill that this girl is missing out on (though there's something to be said for knowing how to do a whole host of things that you never know when you'll need to call on, like working an electric drill, changing a tire, or cutting up a whole chicken into parts, which I'm still not great at even though my mom has tried to show me), but what doing chores *teaches*, such as responsibility, or being a contributing member of a family. And such as finding ways to pay off a debt to parents for those concert tickets or new boots or prom dress you desperately wanted.

Let me take it a step further: It's not just knowing how to wash a car or mow a lawn all by itself, or about the responsibility and entrepreneurship it might teach, but about the feeling of competency and agency and *maturity* that comes with knowing how to do "adult" stuff, and do it well.

Put simply, it makes you feel good. And proud. That's valuable and lasts longer than the nice legs or the ability to do splits (or, to be fair, to hit a double).

Okay, so this sweet young text-happy cheerleader couldn't really wash a car. What else couldn't she do? Did she know how to make a sandwich? Hammer a nail? Boil water for pasta? Dust furniture? Fold a fitted sheet? Plant a tulip bulb? Change a diaper?

Why does it seem that today's kids—speaking broadly here—appear to be growing up in many ways smarter and more worldly and savvy than we did in many cases (hello, Internet!), yet don't know which is the working end of a mop? And just so you don't think I'm all about the chores (who uses mops anymore anyway, with all the Swiffer-y throwaway things? Me, that's who, but I digress), it's about *skills*. It's about kids who get to college and know how to *do* stuff. Who move out on their own and can iron a shirt when it's time for a job interview. Who know how to locate the price-per-pound part of the sticker on the ground beef, or who know about a good melon. And who can come over to their parents' house when they're old and tired and *do stuff* for them.

It's about kids who feel like part of their household, a functioning member of said household, someone who can and does pitch in—and can, *even while complaining about it*—feel that priceless, elusive, "I can do it" feeling.

You know. Pride. So that's why I give you **Mean Mom Manifesto #7: Teach Life Skills. If Not You, Who?** Because too many young people—that cheerleader is just one example—are being sent out into the world knowing how to do all manner of esoteric things, but not always also in possession of useful skills to rely on and, more importantly, without the self-confident pride that comes with it.

Skills? Chores? But Why?!

It's occurred to me that I'm shouting into the wind here. Maybe I'm wrong and no kid really *needs* to learn how to wash a car, do laundry, clean a bathroom, do yard work, or even cook— all things they can have done for them, with enough cash. Shouldn't they spend their time, as young people, studying and playing sports and getting into college, and then later, focus usefully on things like inventing the next super-computer or curing cancer or devising a manned mission to Mars or figuring out why jeans never fit me (just a thought)?

Perhaps. But I still get an uncomfortable feeling when I see teens like this girl demonstrate how incapable they are at basic human stuff, because it's obvious *why* she can't do these things. It's because everything's always been done *for her*. She (and by "she" I mean not just this teen in the short shorts, but many kids these days) has been hovered over since birth. We start out helping our kids cross the street when they're too little to do so on their own, but we skip the part where

> The result seems to be a generation of children with enormous stores of knowledge but few practical skills—and worse, stunted common sense.

we show them how to cross safely on their own, and they never learn, not really.

The result seems to be a generation of children with enormous stores of knowledge but few practical skills—and worse, stunted common sense.

You can just about hear the blades of the parental helicopters beating in the air, can't you? The whole helicopter-parenting dynamic—where parents hover (mostly figuratively, but sometimes literally, such as those parents you see walking just behind their toddlers on the playground, arms outstretched like copter blades) in an attempt to fix and smooth out and protect their kids—has affected this whole generation of children. And one of the things it's done, in my estimation, is made such once-typical aspects of molding and raising children—like teaching them certain skills, like expecting them to tackle certain chores—anachronistic, old-fashioned, even dangerous.

I have friends with sons who are around the same age as my kids. The boys' father (they also recently added a little girl to the family) is big on doing-it-yourself—in the years since he bought their home, he's done serious DIY stuff like new siding, windows, and moving walls around. And he's not reticent about teaching his boys how to do things. They may not be installing drywall (yet), but they can probably tell you what tools you might use.

He also has taught his older boy—who is just a few months older than my son—to mow the lawn. Now, you may think I'm just yammering on here to prove the first point I made in this chapter—that kids should learn these basic life skills, that we should teach them, that they benefit (in the skills themselves as well as the pride) as much as we do. But there's another point that has to do with the helicoptering phenomenon. My friends have told me that when their nine-year-old is out mowing the lawn, neighbors and passersby are taken aback. Some have gone so far as to ask my friends: *How can you let a child mow the lawn?! That's so dangerous!*

To which our friend scoffs. *It's not dangerous*, he tells them before going back to some light work like installing a new garage door or central air conditioning. And he's right. I mean, sure, it *can* be dangerous, but so can skateboarding and so can taking a bath. It's all about perspective. This father has, carefully and responsibly, shown his son how to operate their mower (which like many home lawn mowers these days has built-in safety features anyway); he's impressed on his son proper respect for machinery. He hasn't *shielded* his children from "adult" stuff for fear they'd get hurt.

And let me tell you, the kid practically radiated with pride on the day our friends were telling us this story, and it was not because of the allowance he earns. His chest was puffed up and his blue eyes shone—because *he knew how to mow a lawn!* (And you can bet I sent my own sons out into the yard the next time their dad was doing yardwork, and they've already learned how to pull weeds all the way from the roots, and fill a bag with raked-up leaves.)

So why does it arouse such a collectively negative reaction among some parents to see a nine-year-old out on a sunny Saturday, mowing his family's grass? Why does it even register to other parents as something to take note of? What happened that this generation of parents has not only left out, in many cases, the sharing and teaching of skills as a critical step in parenting but also begun to see it as odd or even dangerous? A few things that I can see:

+ **We got busier.** Or at least, we *felt* busier, so outsourcing what used to be our own parents' normal weekend chores (the ones they eventually taught us to do) became the norm in many circles, things like housecleaning, caring for a backyard pool, mowing the lawn, washing the car, weeding the garden.

+ **We began perceiving the outside world as unacceptably dangerous.** Somehow, it wasn't like that when we were kids, with potential child-snatchers trolling parks and neighborhoods, with giant SUVs zooming down sidewalk-free suburban streets. Some of these perceptions have a basis in reality—the cars, for example; there are just more of them in a more-crowded world. But some of it is false or exaggerated, such as the cable-news-fanned fear of sex offenders on every street corner. Regardless of why, the net result is that there are fewer kids just hanging out playing in streets, backyards, and parks, and more scheduled playdates that kids are driven to.

+ **We took safety concerns to the *n*th degree.** Car seats for babies and booster seats for bigger kids are proven, lifesaving inventions, and safety experts are wise to warn parents that, to use just one example, hot dogs are notorious choking hazards that should be cut up for little kids. But when you're being told left and right what's safe and what's too scary to contemplate, you may have a tendency to just forget trying to figure out when it's 100 percent "safe" to stop cutting up the hot dog. So we keep doing it, or its equivalent (driving them around the corner, staying at the birthday party), long past the time the kid may have the competence and smarts to do it himself. Everything's potentially a safety hazard, right? So we do it all for them, *just in case*.

Danger, Will Robinson!

Sure, as I've said, safety is smart, and perils do exist. *Of course* knives are dangerous when you carelessly leave them in reach of a curious toddler. But what was common sense when your kid was three—that naturally you'll be making her sandwich for her because it's foolhardy to give a preschooler a knife to cut the bread—*remained* common sense when she was seven or eight and perfectly capable of handling at least a butter knife, for heaven's sake, to apply her own peanut butter to her own bread (the mess aside!).

Streets, depending on where you live, can be dangerous and

it wouldn't be smart to, say, send a four-year-old down the block on her bicycle, or ship a first-day kindergartner to the bus stop on his own. But what about when that cycler is seven and in the second grade? At that age (well, actually, in kindergarten even) it never would have occurred to my mother, or possibly yours, to walk me to the bus stop, or to my friend's house, or to speed-walk alongside my bike while I rode. These days, however, all these actions are commonplace.

It's become normal—wait a second, it's become *accepted wisdom*—to look at a second-grader and rather than seeing her growing, potential competence, instead still envision the toddler she used to be, the one who should be kept away from the knife drawer, or the preschooler too oblivious and delicate to ride her bicycle unaccompanied. Not only has viewing our children as helpless and perpetually in danger become received wisdom (and smart parenting), but if you tend to view them in any *other* way (as little people growing in ability and smarts and confidence, as individuals whose competence at certain tasks might be assessed based on their interest and personality), you can be seen as loopy, as cavalier about safety. As bad parents.

But when we hover and worry, we hold our kids back from developing competence and skills on their own. It's like we're waiting for them to demonstrate competence so that we'll feel confident in saying, "Okay, you're old enough now to...[fill in the blank]." But if we're not giving them a chance, or teaching them ourselves, we might have to wait a long time. There's a girl we know who lives across the street from our bus stop, at which there is a stop sign. Granted, plenty of drivers blow right by the sign, but overall it's not too hard to cross that street. She stands there—her parents watching from the front door—hesitating for what seems forever, before setting a foot into the road. She is ten.

Last year I had to *deliberately* teach my third-grader how to stick to the curb as he walks the curving half-block between the bus stop and our house. He can do it, even though I do have to remind him every day to be careful. And yet when I started letting him walk that short stretch solo, I was looked at crookedly and asked more than once by the bus driver if I was sure I didn't want to maybe see about having another bus stop placed in front of my house (that is, once it became clear I wasn't going to trudge up to the stop myself).

Meanwhile, there are middle-school kids being accompanied to the stop by their parents, and no one's giving them the stink-eye.

I'm sure those middle-schoolers can do all kinds of things I couldn't do at their age, like create a website or program a DVR (and it's not just because there was no Web or DVR in my particular Dark Ages). But I also bet they have no idea—since they all have a cell phone and anxious parents—what it's like to sit on the brick retaining wall outside their school, alone, wondering why your mom is fifteen minutes late picking you up, and the school's locked so you can't call from the one payphone in there, and in any case you don't have a dime (yes, a dime). Not that my mom didn't show up—she may have been distracted or stuck in traffic now and then, but she wasn't neglectful. It's just that sometimes she was late, and if she was, well, I cooled my heels. Kids did things like that, cooling their heels. Without supervision.

These days, there's no such thing as no supervision, and certainly no time to cool one's heels. Which leaves no breathing space for a kid to figure out he'd like to be given the freedom to walk home by himself. And which leaves no room for a parent to even realize she's not taught her kid how in any case.

You could argue that the helicopter phenomenon has been joined by the technological revolution (and got mixed in with busier working parents and a more anxiety-ridden economic climate) to produce kids who aren't given a chance to do things. If you're as free-range as most of us were as kids, you figured out how to cross the street, or ride your bike safely to the convenience store for a quart of milk for your mom, because you were *allowed to try.*

And in case you think I've gotten off the **teach them life skills** track here, bear with me: When kids are sheltered and hovered over, they just don't *have* to do stuff, right? And so they never learn. It's chicken and egg leading to another chicken who's too...chicken to cross the street or ride his bike up to the store or pick up the phone to call his piano teacher and tell her he forgot the piece of music he needs for the recital.

So we may be busier, but are we in more danger than before? Popular sentiment, not to mention stories in the news and in viral emails, says we are. But statistics coolly tell us it's the opposite; that, in fact, our children are far safer now than they've ever been in history. And yet we're scared. So we childproof, we hover, we carpool to the bus stop, we arrange activities rather than allow free play.

We want to childproof the world we live in, but here's the rub: The world ain't going away. Our kids do have to live in it some-day—and maybe even change it, dare I say, if they end up with enough gumption to do so. So I have to ask (and it's rhetorical, folks: I know my answer, at least): *Is it better to childproof the world—or to world-proof your child?* (For more on this, see Chapter Ten.)

Taking on the World

And if we decide we'd rather get our kids ready to deal with and manage the world (or at the very least, take on the laundry rooms in their college dormitories), what should we do? **Teach. Them. Life. Skills.**

You've probably heard this, and if so, I'm glad because it's true: Parents are their children's first teachers. No matter what happens later—no matter whether they hit the kindergarten-teacher jackpot—they've got you. We all want to think of our-selves as teachers of our kids, and we all have our "things," the aspects of teaching that most tickle our fancy.

My husband made it a point to show our boys YouTube videos of The Ramones, not just to have fun dancing around to "Teenage Lobotomy" but to share a seminal moment in punk-rock history that shaped my husband's young teens. I remember when our firstborn was a baby and we were eating pizza, happily thinking ahead to the time when we'd teach him how to properly fold a New York slice to most efficiently and neatly consume it. Word-geeky me was thrilled to show my baby boys the right way to hold a book and turn its pages. Now I show them how I work the Sunday *Times* crossword. Well, it shouldn't end there!

We all, to the best of our ability, want to give our children all sorts of lessons, both the kind we can teach them ourselves and the kind we can pay or persuade others to instruct them in. Case in point, the moment we could get our hands on an inexpensive third-hand piano, we grabbed it and I started them on piano lessons, since that's something I've always wished I could do—and because I know how valuable the arts are, and because I'm pretty sure they're not following my footsteps into, say, ballet lessons.

But while we're signing them up for lessons and showing them the inside of a car engine or how a lawn mower works or letting them listen to our favorite bands, let's not forget the most basic of life skills. A boy who can play the piano and name thirty-five different Ramones songs is an awesome kid to know. And when that kid grows up and can also iron a shirt and swish out a toilet bowl (and, to bring it on home here, wash a car)? He's got a leg up on the world, no doubt. He's well on his way to independence. All that, and he can hopefully handle a hot slice of pizza, no problem.

Skills I think every child needs to learn:

Cooking

I should admit, up front, that my parents didn't so much *teach* me how to cook as they did *expect* me (and my siblings) to help.

So I know how to do it, or rather I enjoy the accomplishment and importance of doing it, because of them. (Though I do credit my skill with a chef's knife to the Food Network and Jacques Pepin.) Other useful how-tos gleaned from my folks: washing greens for and then dressing a salad; making a sandwich; stirring sauces so they wouldn't stick to the bottom of the pot; shucking corn; cracking eggs.

My point is that it's not so much about finding out how to make a roux or the best roast chicken ever; that info is available from just about anywhere. It's the feeling that the kitchen is not an alien or off-limits place, but a place you can feel a certain measure of competence. I'm not saying that, if you are strictly a microwave cook or only venture into your kitchen to pull a take-out menu from the drawer, that your kids are doomed, but whatever you do know about feeding them and yourselves? Share it with them. Let them understand how good it feels to know when a meatball is perfectly browned and ready to pop into the simmering sauce (as I learned), or how good it feels to know which is the best sushi place, if that's how you roll (pun intended).

Housework

There's something about staring down a dirty toilet bowl that humbles you. No, really, I mean it. Everyone has a toilet; every toilet gets dirty. It's constant, and it's zen, and when you teach your child the really very simple task of de-crusting the bowl he's spent all week, well, making crusty, you give him power. You think I'm either kidding or vastly overstating my case, but

I am not. Back when I was in my angst-riddled twenties and living on my own, I *swear* I'd feel better after tackling my apartment and turning it from stinky to sparkling. I'm not a clean freak; in fact, I clean far less often than I strictly should. (In our germ-obsessed age, I'm sure I'd fail all sorts of lab tests looking for bacteria on my doorknobs, kitchen counters, or—and I don't like to think about this too much—the sponge. And heaven knows I miserably fail the white-glove test on furniture and moldings.) But knowing that I can turn the situation around at will feels good, and that's a feeling I want my children to have. Let's get back to that humble notion: cleaning our home isn't beneath me, and it shouldn't be either alien or beneath them either.

Yard work

Some years ago, my father went over to my sister's house to do some leaf-raking in a busy season, and recruited my then about sixteen-year-old nephew to help. Later, he marveled to anyone who would listen: "He had no idea how to rake!" He was, apparently, raking the leaves this way, then that way, and eventually getting them into pick-uppable piles, but not *systematically*, as my father had so carefully taught us to do. This is a boy, it should be said, who could pick up virtually any sport he tried with absolute confidence and competence, not to mention grace and coordination. But a rake? A broom? Not so much. It seemed remarkable, and dismaying, to my dad to find that his grandson hadn't been taught the same. Does it matter? I think it does.

You're quite possibly becoming frustrated with me about now, huh? In an age when you can hire out biweekly lawn maintenance for less than it costs to have a daily venti latte, who cares if your kid, or mine, knows how to clean up leaves, shovel snow, run a mower? Your kid will someday as an adult. Again, it's the competence. And it's the pride. When I was growing up, we had a backyard pool, and for a while there my dad did nearly all the tedious maintenance—chemicals, vacuuming, skimming. But once I became a teen, it became my job. I didn't love it at first. No, scratch that. I *never* loved it. But that I knew how the pump and filter system worked? That I knew how to safely handle the chlorine treatments? That I could scoop a stiff dead frog out of the skimmer without yakking up my breakfast? That, dear readers, is *pride*.

> In an age when you can hire out biweekly lawn maintenance for less than it costs to have a daily venti latte, who cares if your kid, or mine, knows how to clean up leaves, shovel snow, run a mower? Your kid will someday as an adult.

Assessing relative safety

Wait, this is a skill? Why, yes, it is! Remember the ten-year-old neighbor girl I mentioned earlier? I begin to believe, as I watch her attempt to cross the street, that she was told—perhaps not officially in words, but via demonstration by well-meaning parents—that all roads have the same degree of relative safety. No matter which one you're crossing, you better have your hand in a parent's vise grip. So what happens is when she's legitimately able to cross the street (and remember, this is the comparatively quiet suburban street, not a four-lane boulevard), she has no internal skill that allows her to assess her own relative safety. If you've always made it so the areas in which your children play are boy-in-the-bubble safe—all rounded edges and recycled-rubber-tires on the ground—if you've always shadowed them on the playground, it's hard for them to judge what's actually safe and what is potentially maybe less so.

A toddler will look up at you before launching down the twisty tunnel slide for the first time (well, most of them will), wordlessly needing your nod of approval. But when that toddler is ten and still looking back over her shoulder to figure out, via her parents' anxious faces, if crossing the street is safe? Something wasn't taught, or hasn't been yet. You have to teach them: You can climb *that* kind of tree, but that chain-link fence with the broken concrete on the far side of it is a less smart climbing structure.

Talking to strangers

I'm an editor by trade, so whenever my kids bring home flyers and other materials from school, my hand reaches for the nearest red pen so I can go to town on mistakes. And it's not just spelling and grammar but *tone* that can make me yearn to edit. Specifics, you ask? Well, let's take the annual efforts in elementary schools to address the "problem" of stranger danger. You're not, these printed materials say, supposed to talk to *anyone* out there, *ever*. So that leaves me in a bit of a quandary. When I tell my sons what to do in case they get separated from me in the mall or at the beach, whom should they talk to? No one? Only a police officer or (if it's at our local upscale mall) a bored-looking security guard tooling around on a Segway? Only moms with strollers? That teaches them to put people into categories. Man on his own? *Do not speak to him under any circumstance!* Man with children? Okay, *maybe*. Woman with stroller? A mom, and therefore above all scrutiny. I say to my kids this: If you're lost, tell someone who looks sympathetic and nice. Go into a store and ask the clerk to help you. At the beach, find the lifeguard stand or just ask...really, almost anyone. Because 99.99999999 percent of folks out there will be nice. It's a skill to trust people—teach it.

Uncomfortable? That's Okay: Why Cooling Your Heels Is a Life Skill, Too

Here's a newsflash for you: Kids are terrible at patience. And waiting. And not being the center of attention. A little illustrative story here: Last spring, we celebrated my older son's First Communion. Arguably, a big deal. He was the guy in the swanky new suit (okay, the inexpensive Target suit, but who's keeping track?), the guy with all eyes on him, the guy with the party in the rented backyard tent and the cake with his name on it. It was *his day*. His little brother? Oh my goodness, he was *jealous*. He was in a mood all day long, and it didn't occur to me until, during a photo session in front of our blooming azaleas with the grandparents, my mother pointed it out. She was surprised herself, but there was the photographic evidence in the tiny screen on the back of my camera.

In *every single photo*, all day long, my younger son had his head down and the most aggrieved puss on his face I've ever seen. Amazing. What did I do? I was tempted to figure out a way to smooth things over for him, but anything that might have had a shot at working would have been ridiculous. Should I abandon my party guests and take him out for an ice cream? He wasn't an infant I had to drop everything to feed; he was a pissed-off five-year-old. So I didn't do much of anything, really. I told him to go and play with his cousins and have fun. Which he did, though he planted that puss on whenever anyone looked at him sideways, especially if they had a camera, you know, in case anyone might catch him having fun. But I was not going to reward that kind of behavior with even a single "poor you."

Mean? No, I don't think so. Mean would have been, "Buck up, short pants; turns out your fears are true and we love the big guy better." Because possibly that's what he was thinking, and my instinct was that if I indulged his 'tude with anything more than a hug and a straightforward acknowledgement of his issue ("I know, everyone's giving your brother gifts, but next time it'll be your turn"), I'd only make his suspicion (which for the record isn't true) feel more possible to him. Instead, I wanted, and hope I managed, to drive home the message that *sometimes it's not your day*. Sometimes it sucks for you. Sometimes you gotta wait. Sometimes the big guy gets all the cool stuff and you get second billing.

So we kept the day's focus on my First Communion boy, knowing that in two years, it would be our little guy's turn to wear the white armband and pose for photos. And if the older guy practices his aggrieved picture face for the day? I'll ignore that, too. And it's not just about big events, of course. Being uncomfortable is part of life, even when you're little, and kids have to learn that...

1. Sometimes the older sibling gets to stay up later.

2. Sometimes the younger sibling gets carried out of the car when he falls asleep (pays to be petite).

3. Sometimes you have to noodle around with a soccer ball on the sidelines because it's not your game today.

4. Sometimes we're at *his* friend's house, not *your* friend's, so you have to either find ways to amuse yourself or—shock! horror!—play with the little sister.

5. Sometimes Grandma doesn't *have* apple juice and you have to drink *water*.

You see my point. Because it's in the un-coddled waiting, the "life isn't always perfectly fair" message, in the times that the sibling sits through the dance recital on the sunny Saturday, that competence and independence are allowed to grow.

[8]

Mean Mom Manifesto #8: Slow It Down. Slow It Way Down.

Hey, moms and dads: what's your rush?

Most of us—but especially those of us who meticulously planned for our children's arrivals—are so sweetly anxious to conceive our babies, bear them, care for them, and dote on them that before they're more than a clump of undifferentiated cells, we've already given them our dad's green eyes or our mom's killer tennis serve, our own love of *Little House on the Prairie* or devotion to the New York Yankees. (In fact, we may already have bought the complete Little House series for the nursery bookshelves—we couldn't resist, even if that felt a wee bit ridiculous—as well as a tiny Yankee-pinstripe onesie and bib.)

We want them *here* already, to be the much anticipated repository of our parental hopes and dreams. There's just one potential problem with all the anticipation: some of us put the whole movie on fast-forward when the early scenes were just building up. As much as we bemoan the speed at which our children grow up (and damn, but it's fast, right?!), we don't do ourselves any favors in that regard, because sometimes we put the whole shebang into hyperdrive, nudging our kids on to the next step and the next and the one after that. And sometimes the consequences aren't all that attractive.

Which is why **Mean Mom Manifesto #8 is Slow It Down. Slow It Way Down.**

Where Are You Rushing To?

We start out with our outsize hopes and dreams being conferred on what's still a clump of cells—someday we'll go to Yankee games together! someday we'll sit and read the *Little House* books together!—and before we know it, that innocent dreaming turns into rushing. We step onto a slippery slope of *growing them up too fast.* Perhaps impatient to enjoy things with them, we take them to every G-rated movie that comes out and quickly move on (after we've bought the DVDs of everything they've seen already) to the PGs. After all, even though he's only five,

> Sometimes we put the whole shebang into hyperdrive, nudging our kids on to the next step and the next and the one after that. And sometimes the consequences aren't all that attractive.

he loves *Transformers* or *Captain America.* (But does he really, or is it that he saw a Transformers toy hawked on a cereal box?)

By age six, you can't just run to Target and grab two-for-$10 plain old T-shirts because your savvy little customer wants Justice or (I shudder to think) Abercrombie. (And because she seems to want it so much, or because you're not in the mood to argue your position or don't think she'll understand it, or because you have a niggling fear she won't feel cool if you deny her the Justice, you give in.)

These things are not inborn in our children; no one comes out of the womb either super-acquisitive or (worse yet) blasé about clothes, movies, toys, sports events, and at-home privileges. It starts with *us* pushing *them*. Knowingly or not, we can create and then foster in our kids the sense that what is right in hand and either age-appropriate or possibly slightly less so (such as girls playing with baby dolls when they're still in first grade or even later) is *not good enough*, because there's something else bigger and better and more sophisticated. It's like we see a little girl playing with a baby doll at five and instead of thinking, "Oh, how sweet; she still plays little mama with her baby doll," we think, "Time to get her a high-fashion Barbie!" Or it may be someone else doing the thinking—a grandparent, an aunt, a friend—and they show up at the next birthday with the latest super-cool (and possibly squeamishly sexy) doll in the brazen miniskirt. For some reason, the trend has shifted from keeping kids innocently interested in the pint-size carriage or teddy-bear tea parties *as long as we possibly can* to deliberately getting preschoolers intrigued by lip gloss and Justin Bieber. (Or Justin Bieber lip gloss; does that exist? I wouldn't be a bit surprised.)

I'm sorry: did we want our children to be sophisticated cultural consumers at five? Or do we just think those Justin Bieber T-shirts are just too cute? Or is it that we get some sort of hard-to-shake feeling that if we miss some sort of cultural moment (the latest hotshot singer, a movie, a toy, an experience), our kids will end up left out, behind?

Shouldn't they be playing with worms in the backyard instead? I think that in a romantic, oh-isn't-childhood-so-innocent sense, then yes, we *do* pay lip service to the idea of keeping kids *kids* for longer, chasing fireflies at dusk on summer nights, playing flashlight tag, reading *The Hardy Boys* under a blanket tent, begging for change for the ice-cream vendor, sledding down the hill at the park, feeding the ducks in the local pond (all these being true of my childhood, except for *Hardy Boys*; I was a Nancy Drew girl). And yet we often don't do those things. Oh, we may do these specific things or similar ones or encourage our kids to do them. But we also do all the other things, taking them (sometimes joylessly, as though it were a job) to the latest shoot-'em-up movie, buying whatever the latest gadget is *just because it's there*.

And then we sigh sadly that their childhood disappears so quickly.

> Is it that we get some sort of hard-to-shake feeling that if we miss some sort of cultural moment...our kids will end up left out, behind?

What's Next?!

Many of today's parents—in unintended collusion with the endless marketing of *stuff*, much of which is inappropriate for young children—constantly shuffle their kids to the next and the next and then the next *thing*. So you've got the four-year-old with the "I'm Your Future Lawsuit" T-shirt ("Isn't it cute?!"); the eight-year-old with the iPad 2 ("Well, her *sister* got one"); the ten-year-old who *has* to stay up past 10:00 p.m. to watch *Man Vs. Wild* or to vote for her favorite *American Idol* contestant ("But they love it! What can I do?"); the fourteen-year-old with the prom dress that wouldn't be out of place on the Oscar red carpet ("Yes, it cost a mortgage payment, but doesn't she look like a star? Wait, stop looking at her cleavage!"); and that girl's sixteen-year-old prom date, who happens to be packing vodka in his Poland Spring bottle in the limo ("I know, but they all do it...").

Some might argue (and they do; I've heard them!) that the kids will get these things and see these things and do these things no matter what we do, so isn't it better if they do, see, and get these things with our knowledge, even with our permission? Isn't it better they see we're on their side, that we're their pal? That way, they're not sneaking around. And some would say they just don't want their children left out of the game. Or that, in the case of things that seem harmless or even amusing (like ironically sexy T-shirts for kindergartners), *who wants to be the prude*?

But that's backward thinking. That's retrofitting your parenting style—your values—to the prevailing culture, when it should be the other way around. Let the world zoom by for other kids, other families; it's up to you to decide how fast you want your children to grow up. (And I hope your decision will be to Slow. It. Down.)

Slowing down is not just about the stuff (more on that later!) but also about the attitude. This is probably highly old-fashioned of me (big surprise), but I don't believe in giving kids things before they ask for them, and certainly not before they need them. I also don't happen to believe in pushing them to the next thing when it *doesn't* necessarily have to do with stuff (like technology or toys or whatever) but when it simply has to do with an attitude, a way of thinking, a way of acting. I say, keep the innocence as long as you can. They're kids for a blink—but they'll be adults for a long, long lifetime.

> Let the world zoom by for other kids, other families; it's up to you to decide how fast you want your children to grow up.

And when they do get around to asking, when their consciousness has risen to the point where, say, they notice what's out there, what's available, what others have? *Then* you make the yay-or-nay decision—and yes, you can still use the "nay." I'm going to toss out a few examples of what I mean. See if you can figure out what they all have in common:

The case of the buttercream frosting

I'm at a family party. My firstborn is still less than a year old, it's evening, and he's been changed out of his party outfit and into a white terrycloth onesie. The wife of a distant cousin of mine is holding her own baby son on her lap at the dining-room table; the boy is around my son's age, give or take a month. The table is groaning with dessert (typical of family parties; it's how we roll, and I mean that literally). Guests are sampling this and that, slicing an edge off that cake and passing over a wedge of that pie and grabbing another cookie or piece of chocolate from trays. And this mom says, "What can I give him? Let's see..." And before long, someone's quickly cut her a piece of sheet cake for the baby. He can't eat it himself, but she scoops a fingerful of buttercream off the top to put to his lips. My son? In the white onesie? He's crawling around, completely oblivious to dessert. Let me tell you, eight-plus years later, he's moved from oblivious to utterly devoted when it comes to dessert— but he got there *on his own*. No way was I starting with a finger full of cream when he was eight months old.

See, I knew he'd get there; I was not, and am not now, against dessert, in moderation (except at parties, where moderation is checked at the door). But my polite refusal of "a cookie for the baby?" when he was a baby and immune to the cookie's lure was often taken for a lifelong anti-dessert stance. Not so—but neither did I want to *rush him* into the wonders of buttercream and chocolate. Or soda. Don't get me started on *that*.

The case of the iPod Touch

I'm chatting amiably with a local mom, someone I know slightly from the soccer circuit. Soon enough, another mom, one I don't know, rushes up, late to meet the first mom. She is clutching a Best Buy shopping bag, apologizing for her tardiness. *"What a day! After work, I had to rush over to Target and return the iPod I got Halley for Christmas, and then buy another one at Best Buy."*

Um, what? I'll spare you the detailed script of the head-swiveling back-and-forth I ended up being party to, but suffice to say that Halley—a second-grader—had *really* wanted a Flip video camera, but then her mom realized that the iPod also had video capability and...I forget what other reason there would be to get an eight-year-old this sophisticated gadget. Just for making goofy videos with her friends? Because you're sick of her begging to borrow yours to play Angry Birds? Who knows. But anyway, the one she'd originally bought at Target was fine, but then she saw an ad for Best Buy offering a free $25 gift card if you bought the phone with them—Hey! What a deal!—so she did the two extra errands and felt ahead of the game. I'll say she was ahead of the game, because my question (which I didn't ask out loud) was, "What does Halley get next year? A Lexus?" And in case you were wondering, the other mom, whose son is friends with Halley, was furious with her friend for upping the peer-pressure ante: "Now Brandon will want one, too!"

The case of the long-beloved *Little Bear*

I'm watching a commercial for the latest Disney movie and wondering why so many of them are PG and so few are G. I think I know the answer, in part: Movies that used to be made for kids and *just* for kids were mind-numbing for parents. But *Kung Fu Panda II*? That's sufficiently entertaining (or is meant to be) for the adults too. I've read that the prime moviegoing audience is adolescent males. Well, it seems even the purportedly kid movies are made to appeal to that subset; adult movies dumbed down, kid movies tarted up, all to meet somewhere in a perpetual-adolescent middle.

Don't misread me here: I *like* that so-called family movies have enough inside jokes, pop culture references, familiar actors providing voices, and—above all—snark to keep me from fleeing my seat for another tub of 4,000-calorie popcorn. But when my kids were really little—under five, say, or even, given their relative indifference for such a long time to movies, and their lack of access to commercial TV for a blessed while there, under six or seven—there really wasn't a movie I felt I wanted to take them to. Or, there wasn't a movie that—this is key—they'd really like. Not having brought them to the movies hadn't been a thought-out plan of ours; it happened mostly because our firstborn had some issues with loud noises, so even a lion puppet playing a saxophone in a Baby Einstein video freaked him out. Dolby surround sound plus darkness would have sent him around the bend.

So when he, and then his brother, started watching TV, it was Noggin (now Nick Jr.), and it was ideal. Shows like the lovely *Little Bear*, the annoying *Franklin*, the weird and fun *Maisy*, the lisping *Wonder Pets*, the delightful *Backyardigans*, and many other favorites, were all about twenty-five minutes long, with no commercials for movies or toys or cereal. My boys' Noggin phase lasted a *long* time, while movies slipped by somewhere beyond their consciousness. Even DVDs of older favorites didn't capture their attention.

There was a point, though, at which my sister said, "You know, you should ditch the Noggin and take them to a Disney movie." But—and I said this to her—why? Until they turn away from *Little Bear* on their own (and they most assuredly and sadly did), I'm not going to turn them off; I'm not going to tell my children that five is "too old" to watch *Little Bear*. One time, my parents were over when *Little Bear* was on, and at one point, everyone left the room for one reason or another but for my dad. When we came back, the show was still on and I said to my father, "Dad, you could have changed the channel!" His reply, with a shrug and a smile: "It's a nice show." Indeed, it is.

Did you see what these scenarios all have in common? Parental notions that, somehow, something isn't moving fast enough, so we should nudge it ahead for our kids.

The buttercream frosting mom? She was looking for a dessert she could pop into the mouth of an infant who hadn't *asked* for dessert: *what's her rush?* I suspect she hadn't really thought about it, but just sort of vaguely felt that sometime in the near future, she'd have an older kid pulling on her arm and asking for a cupcake or some ice cream, so why not start now? Not to mention, who gets to be the cool mom? The one with the buttercream, of course. Or the one who distractedly says *yes* to the Coke for the three-year-old.

The iPod Touch mom? She felt it necessary to buy her eight-year-old an iPod Touch, not because the girl had some overachieving, preternaturally advanced affinity for technology, but because the iPod was, well, *there* (not to mention on sale). *What's her rush?* What I saw there was a raging case of Jones-keeping-up-itis, don't you think? That poor woman was racing all over town, trying to get the best deal on an item that *her daughter had not asked for*, and then spent a good ten minutes nervously justifying her purchase to her stony-faced friend, who was herself more concerned with the peer pressure situation this would stimulate between Little Miss iPod and her own, presumably less electronically endowed, son.

And the moms who itch to ditch *Little Bear*? What's the rush to *Kung Fu Panda II*? *Why rush them*? Well, of course, I didn't push them off Noggin; they got there on their own, figured out that less sweetly calming TV fare lurked on other channels. But I still have to wonder: what makes some parents, some *people* actually, antsy and uncomfortable when they see little kids *not growing up fast enough*? Why is he still watching *Little Bear*?! Why does she still play with dolls?

I'm not sure why—though I suspect it has to do with this idea that growing them up faster gives them an edge in a more fast-paced world (as though there's some sort of line between a kid who knows all the latest superhero movies in first grade and, say, Yale). But my answer to those panicky, *why does he still watch Noggin* questions is simple: why not?

How to Slow...It...Down.

The thing about applying the grow-up brakes is it takes active work. You have to make decisions like "I won't offer him soda or cupcakes and candy before he asks. When he asks? Eh, we'll think about it again then." You have to strategize: "If I get them a computer, I'll have to come up with a system for sharing of time between siblings, and possibly break out the kitchen timer." You have to make short-term rules: "You can watch TV or play video games in the hour between homework and dinner, but not after, when we practice instruments or go for a family walk." And you have to make long-term rules: "Yes on the computer and the other tech as time goes on, but until you're in a college dorm, there will not be a computer in your room, period."

I'm not saying these specific rules have to be yours, but you have to do *something* to create boundaries; otherwise, all you're doing is throwing stuff at them and leaving it to them to sort out. And we all know from watching little kids with a stack of presents at Christmas or on their birthdays: if you throw things at kids, they tear them open, toss them aside, and look for what's next.

> Once you say *yes* to a jump ahead in treats or privileges, you can't go back, not without an uphill battle.

You also have to be willing to brush off or ignore parental peer pressure. Huh, you ask? Yes, pressure from *other parents* to speed things up, give in, give up, give the kid something, from a can of soda (when he's eighteen months old) to...well, an iPod Touch at his seventh birthday. I call it the "oh, just give him a cookie" factor. Here's a story: When my husband's nephew was about one, another aunt of his asked, at a party, if she could give the boy a sip of her soda. I'm not sure if either of the boy's parents actually said *yes* specifically, but perhaps this woman felt she'd gotten the nod. She gave the child a sip of her Coke. Half an hour later, she said, "He keeps following me! He wants more!" Um, yes, he does. Of course he does. Coke is *sweet*. Kids like sweet. And once you say *yes* to a jump ahead in treats or privileges, you can't go back, not without an uphill battle.

Of course, in this example, it wasn't exactly another parent giving you the eye-roll. (Why won't she just give the kid a cup of soda? She's such a hard-ass!) But maybe you have seen that happen or have experienced it yourself. You *want* to stick to your guns—you've told the kids *no* to the ubiquitous ice-cream truck at the soccer field—but then the other parents are doing it. And not just doing it, but chiding *you* for *not* doing it. It's lighthearted on the outside, but what it really comes down to is this: if these other parents see you giving in and getting your kids the ice cream too, you're helping to validate their choice. If you don't get the ice cream (or whatever's at stake), you leave those other parents feeling either defensive or dragged kicking and screaming (mentally, not actually) into evaluating their own choice. Most parents simply don't want to confront their choices—finding it easier to give in because they want to be the child's go-to, high-fiving, ice-cream-buying best pal, that old path-of-least-resistance thing.

So, what does parental peer pressure have to do with slowing down? And what the heck is wrong with some ice cream? A lot, and nothing (in some cases). Parental peer pressure isn't just about ice cream on the soccer field before lunch. It spills over, it grows like weeds, and before you know it, you're getting the stink-eye if you're the boring, stick-in-the-mud, problem-causing parent who won't let your kid come over when there's no adult in the house or won't drive the thirteen-year-olds to the R-rated movie, who won't let the high schoolers drink at your house. The stakes keep getting higher, and the higher they get, the faster things go.

It's "slow down," not "go back in time"

When I say "slow down," I want to be clear I'm not necessarily talking about going back to Mayberry. I do understand that time marches on, that children progress with each generation in savvy and smarts that exceed their parents'. I also understand that, as parents, you *do* have to spend some time keeping up and preparing your children for the ever more complex world you've brought them into. My kids use computers in school; when they wanted one of their own at home, it would have been daffy of me to suggest they try my old typewriter instead.

And while I'm on the subject of technology bugaboo, let me go back to the example of the iPod Touch. I still firmly believe that the parent I saw that day, weeks before Christmas, clutching her Best Buy bag, had jumped the "she's ready for this" gun by a bit. (I knew it myself, but it was confirmed by the other mother's reaction, *and* by the iPod mother's reaction to that reaction. She doubted her decision—I could tell by how limply she defended it.) That said, I'm *not* arguing that there's some magical age that a child is "ready" for the next bit of tech. I know there are ten-year-olds who can take an iPad and compose music with it, which is ten different kinds of awesome.

Advancing the tech your kids have should not be a matter of "It's there! Buy it! Her friend Katie has it!" It should instead be made individually and rationally. My cousin pointed this out to me recently, reminding me that his parents got him what was then the equivalent of an iPad (some very, very early personal computer whose name I don't recall) when he was considerably younger than the usual owner of such expensive, untested tech. But they knew his interest wasn't just in having something cooler or newer than the next kid; it was actual, serious interest in computers, and it's paid off, given that this cousin now owns a successful software company.

I get it: without question, I am not a Luddite pining for the days when kids used slates and chalk. Technology is a part of our kids' world, far more than anyone thought back in the early 1980s, when my parents bought my little brother the Commodore 64 computer and we played Pong on our Atari video game. Or in the late '80s when, as a senior in college, I got an Apple Mac Plus to replace my until-then-fancy electronic typewriter. My parents, though, weren't buying me that computer because it was the "thing" or so I would look cool in the dorm (that ship had long ago sailed, unfortunately!) but because I was an English major pounding out twenty-page papers on a weekly basis and gearing up to write a thesis. ("If you're going to be a writer, I guess you're going to need one of these," my father said presciently.)

I confess all this rush-rush feeling around raising kids—not to mention how complicit many of us are as parents in the rushing—has left me puzzled and a little sad. Here we are, this whole generation of bright, educated, healthy, and (mostly) solvent parents, so anxious to have and then dote on our babies, to give them what we perhaps didn't have both materially and emotionally. How and why did that positive impulse get all muddled up into a compulsive, competitive effort to push our kids to the next step, the next thing? We're so determined, aren't we?

Our hurrying takes a few different forms. See if anything's familiar to you:

+ We want to **expose our kids to things**: movies, TV shows, products, technology. So they can keep up with their peers? So *we* can keep up with *our* peers?

+ We want to **hasten them out of the baby phase,** bundling away "little kid" toys to make room for handheld video games and the like. Because we're made uncomfortable by a child who is diapering a baby doll at seven, rather than hip-swiveling her way through a Miley Cyrus CD?

+ We perhaps want to **head off dangerous behavior** that might be coming around the bend as they do get older—like drinking—by acting all cool-parent and letting young teens imbibe at home parties.

+ We want to **be an easygoing friend** more than we care to be a parent wrestling with tough choices, so we allow unfettered Internet access, or Facebook pages for which we don't know the password.

Staying Happy with the Here and Now

I'll say it again: every time you rush things ahead, you're in effect throwing up your hands. You're saying, "They'll get there anyway, why not right now?" Do we realize that if we keep throwing our kids the next thing, they'll end up, you know, *expecting the next thing*? Not being content with what they already have? So then the question becomes: *how do you slow yourselves down in a world that's rushing by*? Imagine you're standing beside a fast river with your kids, a river of stuff and experiences and things that'll hasten their growing up. How do you pick the things you think are best for them without the river threatening to sweep them up and carry them too fast downstream? Here are some slow-it-down strategies:

Don't let them decide

It's easy to place the "blame" on the kids themselves: "Hey, it's my kid who keeps pushing for more sophistication and maturity!" It's not *you* that's pushing them to grow up! *They* want it! *They* are agitating (mercilessly) for stuff that's perhaps not suited for their age or pressing for privileges you feel are ill-suited to their age, such as staying up later at night, seeing movies too suggestive or too violent for them, getting a cell phone (or a better/smarter phone), or *whatever* it is that represents "I'm bigger now." And it's certainly true that as kids grow up—especially once they reach whatever age it is for them that they can *feel* themselves growing up (for me it was ten)—they'll start asking for changes that suit their newly more mature status.

And yet, isn't it still at least mostly up to you? My kids saw a commercial last holiday season for something called a Ground Force Drifter, which seemed to be some kind of very souped-up version of a child's Power Wheels–type toy or a slightly scaled-down version of an engine-powered go-kart. Let's just say *no way* any eight- and six-year-olds in my house were getting anywhere near that (and they are *expensive*). Obviously they didn't *need* a Ground Force Drifter. I'd argue they didn't even really want it, not in that way that an astute parent can sense when a child really, *really* wants something and demonstrates he's ready for it or that he won't abuse the privilege of getting it or get prematurely bored with it. You, the parent, have to hone your sense of when your child—your individual child—is ready for what he's asking for. Not him. They ask, of course; that's their job. But if we grant them those changes in status earlier, all we're doing is setting the "I'm ready for more" alarm earlier and earlier, so you have two-year-olds with Barbies instead of baby dolls and six-year-olds zooming around in a Ground Force Drifter rather than, you know, a *bicycle*.

Recognize (and reject) peer pressure

Not long ago, I spoke to a friend who has twelve-year-old twins, a boy and a girl. She had just come from shopping for a dress for the sixth-grade dance that would meet her daughter's approval as well as her own. There are slim pickings out there in that narrow range, apparently, and what her daughter *wanted* was, as my friend called it, "a hooker dress." (Unfortunately, super-short, tight, spangly frocks are all the rage in middle school.) For now, my pal is sticking to her "no hooker dresses" guns, but she admits it's not easy—and this is a mom I'd define as pretty tough. But the pressure—from her daughter, from her daughter's friends, and even from her daughter's friends' *mothers*—is palpable and harder to resist.

But resist you have to. Which doesn't mean you have to draw every line in every stretch of sand you come across with your kids; there is, and should be, plenty of room for negotiation, depending on the situation and your child's age. Resisting peer pressure should be something you muster the presence of mind to do for long enough to dispassionately view the situation at hand, weigh it, and then make choices that sit well with you. Take my friend and the hooker dress: though she won't buy a dress that barely covers her child's prepubescent figure, neither will she insist on a floor-length, high-necked dress an Amish mom would approve *just* for the sake of resisting peer pressure.

Teach them about marketing and advertising

Most of us, to our credit, aren't buying all the crap our kids see on TV or in their friends' homes. But I'd argue that not enough of us are *explaining why* to our kids. The answer is either, "Oh, sure, we can get that," or "No way, José," but what's missing there is an opportunity to discuss *why* the answer is *no*. Or even *yes*.

My boys only started watching commercial TV relatively recently. (Oh, Noggin, how I miss you!) As you might imagine, they were total blank slates as far as advertising's siren pull. "Mom! Mom! You *have* to get this Oxy Foam Cleaner stuff! You spray it all over the bathroom, and it just *sparkles!*" I got a good laugh out of that one, but a little alarm went off when I witnessed their complete faith that whatever was said on TV had to be true. Like this one: "Mom, can we get Lucky Charms? They're part of a complete breakfast!" (And as an aside, isn't it funny that the sugary-cereal commercials continue to trot out that "complete breakfast" line, a generation after I heard it on TV myself? Kills me.) I had to explain to them what "complete breakfast" really means. I told them, "Listen, we can sometimes get some kinds of cereals like that, but we'll get them for fun, not because they're part of a good breakfast—because they're *not*."

As adults, we may take it as a matter of course that TV commercials...let's say, stretch the literal truth, or put a high polish on things they're hawking in an effort to make you feel somehow incomplete if you don't *have* it. But our kids don't have that awareness—and it's our job, if we want to keep them from growing up in a rush, to teach them. Funny, isn't it, that teaching them greater awareness, irony, skepticism—all pretty grown-up concepts—can be used to keep them younger, but it works. Or anyway, it keeps Ground Force Drifters from showing up under your Christmas tree!

A final thought on marketing and advertising aimed at kids: just because it's ubiquitous doesn't mean we lie down in front of that particular train.

Practice saying, "This is what we do"

"But *Tommy* got the Ground Force Drifter." "Mom, you know, Caitlin gets to stay up until 9:00 on school nights, and *as late as she wants* on the weekends!" Sigh. It was ever thus: kids press to be given more and greater privileges or things and use whatever ammunition they can gather, including in large measure what other kids are allowed. You can't stop this. I'm convinced there was a cave-kid complaining that some other cave-kid pals could hunt mammoth on their own and why did his parents make him stay home in the cave like a baby? So yeah, you can't *stop* your kids from comparing her privileges and the contents of her toybox or electronic stash with that of her friends. What you can do is make clear what *your* parameters, values, and rules are.

It sounds almost comically simple, but it really is true. I got the stay-up-later push-back from my older guy last year, when he reported back what a same-age girl at his bus stop was allowed to do, namely, choose her own bedtime. I was tempted to talk about what was wrong about that in the other family, but then I realized: it's not about the other family; it's about ours. So I said,

"Listen, honey, I get it, but this is what we do in our house. You stay up a little later on weekends, and when you get a bit older, we'll talk about it again." He still grumbled, but he heard me.

Define your own bottom-line values

Holding fast to your principles as they strain against your child's strong will to grow up as fast as she can is hard, but it's still our task, isn't it? I told the story, earlier in this chapter, of the mom who bought the iPod Touch for her second-grader and seemed to me to have not thought it through. She was reacting—in this case, to a combination of a good sale at Best Buy and the notion that the girl would go nuts with happiness over such a gift. But our job is not to react, at least not all the time. It's our job to anticipate. And to do that we have to decide what our values are.

This is where strict religious or cultural mores make it sort of easy. If you're Amish, you're not wondering if you should buy an iPod now or wait until the child is older (that whole "no electricity" thing really takes a lot out of the decision process). But just because the majority of us don't have that formal code to go by doesn't mean we don't have to create one for ourselves, with whatever rules and parameters (strict ones, loose ones) feel comfortable for us.

No Pushing, Please!

I'm not breaking any ground by saying we live in a fast world: everything's at your fingertips, literally in the case of the ubiquitous touchscreen. That said, I'd argue every generation of parents has felt the pull of society moving faster than they remembered as kids—that's just human nature. Reminds me of an episode of *Little Bear*, to bring that lovable little cartoon friend up again. Mother Bear and Father Bear go to "the city" for the day, and when they return, Mother Bear talks wonderingly about how much the metropolis had changed: "You can't stop progress!" she says with a laugh before tucking into some cake and lemonade.

True enough, Mother Bear; you can't stop progress, but you can keep the parts of it that you don't agree with, or not yet, at bay.

And if you are about to say that part of being a good parent is giving your kids more than you got, I hear you, and I do it too. But be sure that you're doing it, or giving it, or providing it, because it fits with your values and your budget. Do it because it feels right, rather than in a misguided attempt to help your child "keep up" or in an equally misguided attempt to "be cool" in your kids' eyes.

Then there's the "they'll get there soon enough on their own anyway" argument for rushing growing up. And yes, it's true they'll get there soon enough. But if we rush them there, they'll be there for a lot longer, "there" being adulthood. Let 'em be kids. Let 'em wear regular T-shirts, not ones with irony that they don't get, and regular dresses, not belly shirts that say "Don't you wish your daughter was hot like me?" (Not sure that exists, actually. Wait, I hope that one doesn't exist!)

I've noticed that many parents appear to believe that modern-day kids "get it"; they're savvier by nature, less innocent, and so can "handle" more sophisticated entertainment or other offerings. I don't buy it. Kids are kids. But if you are in thrall to that belief—if you see that the world is fast and scary and full of messes tailor-made for kids to get into—you may push your kids ahead in an effort to help them. So you nudge him up a few notches on the maturity ladder, and voilá, he appears to be able to go with the flow on everything from a scary movie to a late bedtime to a roomful of tech even you don't have. Sure, he appears to: kids can "play" mature long before they actually are. (Think of all those prepubescent girls working their short skirts and belly shirts—they act sexy before they have any real idea what "sexy" is.)

Life moves fast enough on its own. Let's not press fast-forward, okay?

Oh, Baby. Dolls.

I rarely think about dolls any longer, which stands to reason, given I live in what I call Denise's House of Penises. The closest we get to dolls is the Hulk figurine that came either from a Happy Meal or a goody bag. Anyway, I played with dolls all the time as a child, baby dolls at first, then Barbies. My Newborn Baby Tender Love was very well cared for and had very sweet custom clothes—drawstring nighties, cotton rompers, and pantaloons with rickrack trim—thanks to my grandmother, a seamstress. I kept at doll-playing for a long time, which was fairly typical back then, moving from baby dolls to Barbies by what would today be called my "tween" years. (Eight, maybe? These days, Barbies are adopted and discarded practically before kindergarten.) And yes, my Barbies had awesome handmade wardrobes too, including a gold lamé evening gown, a wedding dress, and a super-chic '70s mini-dress, all made from scraps of the clothes my grandmother crafted for herself. Anyway, no one was rushing me away from caring for my dolls, and no one worried that I was no longer still a baby myself and should do something more sophisticated (like what, date?).

In the era in which I grew up, not rushing daughters away from baby dolls was normal (same with not rushing boys away from playing with trains and dump trucks). But I had the added wrinkle (a welcome wrinkle, to me) of having been raised by a mother who admits to having played with her own baby doll for so long (age fourteen was when she finally, reluctantly, put away the little carriage she pushed her doll in) that she felt almost startled when, at age twenty—a mere six years later—she was pushing a real carriage around, with a real baby (my sister) inside. But you know what? Playing with dolls for longer than most of today's parents might stomach did not turn her into some sort of immature freak; in fact, I contend it did the opposite. When real life called—in the guise of a young marriage, an apartment of her own, and a baby— she stepped up.

Meanwhile, and by contrast, it seems to me we push and push and pile on the too-sophisticated stuff and activity on our kids in some misguided effort to grow them up fast, and we end up with the opposite. That second-grader, earlier in this chapter, who opened up an iPod Touch last Christmas? She may be more likely to pack away her dolls earlier than I was at that age, but we shouldn't be confused as parents into thinking that holding a sophisticated adult piece of tech automatically confers maturity. It doesn't, any more than a fourteen-year-old playing with a baby doll automatically means a child is too babyish.

[9]

Mean Mom Manifesto #9:
Fail Your Child, a Little Bit,
Every Day.

I t's fair to say that parents don't get into this whole
having-and-raising-kids game expecting to *fail*. Our
hopes are too high, our plans too grand, our intentions
too pure (at least, at the very beginning of our first pregnancies!). I'd argue no parent ever had failure in mind at
the get-go, but what used to be, back in the beginning of
human-hood, a matter of mere survival turned into something those early ancestors wouldn't even recognize as
parenting today. For evidence of this, you need not look all
the way back into fuzzy human history to our not-totally-
upright forbears. You only have to travel back two or three
generations to see the change in definition of "success" or
"failure" at parenting as radically, wildly different.

Take my grandparents' generation. For them, success was
often a matter of the child surviving past toddlerhood; most
of the rest was gravy.

Here's an example of what I mean, contained in one family—my father's. My father was born in 1936. He was the first-born of his then-mid-twenties-age parents, and he was *beyond* beloved. But my grandparents were struggling. They lived upstairs in my grandmother's parents' house, with her younger, single sisters underfoot. All fairly typical for the time, the extended family, the "village." My father was frequently ill as a child, and this before the invention of life-saving antibiotics, so the fact that he made it past a scary bout of pneumonia as a school-age child was attributed, mainly by my grandmother, to countless candles lit in church and prayers offered up to Mother Cabrini. The pediatrician, the ubiquitous Dr. Scholnick, was there (complete with cigarette clamped between his lips on house calls), but he could do little more than my grandmother and her gaggle of sisters. (Talk about an era in which experts were *not* king; in fact, they were often no more helpful, and certainly not more relied upon, than instinct, family, common sense, and long-held belief and practices.)

When he wasn't busy being life-threateningly ill, my dad was either in school or outside playing stickball in the vacant lots of Brooklyn, running free in the neighborhood, going to his aunt's house to get slices of bread spread with butter and sprinkled with sugar. My point is that once my father was no longer a baby and was deemed more or less healthy, he was largely on his own, as long as he dressed warmly enough (though in my grandmother's opinion, her children and later her grandchildren were never dressed warmly enough!), was respectful, and came home for meals. The same went for his sister, born four years after him (with important caveats; being a girl, she had far less freedom than my father did, but that's another book).

My grandparents had *hopes* for their children, sure, but being rewarded with children who survived childhood, ate what was put in front of them, went to school, and didn't talk back to their parents was already more than they'd hoped for (well, for grandchildren, too, I suppose, and they got those soon enough).

But fast-forward to 1950. My grandmother found herself pregnant a final time, her "surprise" child, my Baby Boomer uncle. By then, the game had changed, because the times had changed. My grandparents were older, more solvent. They'd bought a small house, moving "up" from stickball, vacant-lot Brooklyn to rose-bushes-by-the-garage Queens. My grandfather had a good government job and spent his daily nickel (literally) to travel by subway to downtown Manhattan, in his overcoat and fedora. My grandmother stayed home and, well, kind of got fat.

They were different parents in 1950 than they were in 1936. Now, I'm not saying my grandmother acted like the type of parent you'd see today (for one thing, no one had invented Gymboree yet), but she was for sure more involved and more invested in the raising of her third baby. No longer was it about compelling this, her youngest, to eat the broccoli even though it still had a few bugs squirming around in it ("be quiet and eat it; it's protein"). It was about making sure he had books to read. It was money saved for college. Some of this had to do with the fact that they were veteran parents by then, and that they had help in caring for the littlest one in the form of his fourteen- and ten-year-old siblings. This meant that my grandmother, instead of praying to Mother Cabrini and trying to afford enough bug-infested broccoli for the family, could sort of relax and actually pay less-divided attention to her youngest.

You can argue about whether my young uncle was spoiled, but it's pretty clear that my grandparents' child-rearing attitude had shifted. It wasn't about survival anymore. It was about depositing on my uncle all kinds of hopes and dreams they probably hadn't dared to have before. Whereas early in their parenting career my grandparents wanted their kids to *live*, their later efforts were all about wanting their youngest son to *thrive*.

More recently—in our own childhoods, for the most part—the fail-or-not benchmark was roughly drawn around "Can I get this kid up and out of my house, with a basic education and ability to support herself, by the time she's eighteen-ish?" Accomplish that (have a child with four limbs and a beating heart; have a child who tips herself out of the nest while you still have some life left in you), and you, you know, *didn't fail*.

Now, I'm not saying that my grandparents did a better job with my dad than with my uncle, or even the opposite. What I am saying is that since the first inklings of the kind of focus-on-the-child parenting style (not just his survival, but his emotional, social, educational, and psychological needs), which my grandmother experienced in her second "shift" as a mother, change accelerated rapidly. That change—the greater emphasis on the child—meant it was harder for parents to accept the whole idea of *failure*. The idea that sometimes, you *do* fail, even in little ways.

And that sometimes, those failures *are good things for your child.*

Thinking about failure (and what's good about it, even if at first that seems terribly counterintuitive to a well-meaning, earnest parent of today) is what helped me develop **Mean Mom Manifesto #9: Fail Your Child, a Little Bit, Every Day.**

Parenting = Precious

Parents have always loved their kids, no news there. And they've always found them precious. (I remember my cousin saying to me, when one of her daughters was being particularly trying and she was struggling to find a silver lining, "What can I do? She's my most precious thing.") But these days, our children feel somehow more precious than they once were.

They are not simply precious in the sense of "Oh, that baby's thighs are just too precious." Instead they are precious in that they are somehow inherently fragile. Rare. Make or break. This child is not solely the life you brought into your house and have the responsibility to raise as best you can.

> Whereas it used to be immensely important to care for our children so that they *lived,* now it's immensely important to care for our children *because our children reflect us.*

As I mentioned earlier in the book, this child is now *your project.*

Whereas it used to be immensely important to care for our children so that they *lived,* now it's immensely important to care for our children *because our children reflect us.* And that's a job at which we simply cannot fail.

Where does that leave us? In a curious place where we feel compelled to do everything, both with and for our children, in an effort to keep them ahead of the pack, on top of their game—and to keep ourselves ahead of and on top of some perceived excellent-parent scale. It's no longer just about keeping them alive and taking care of the basics—whatever your grandparents' and parents' definition of "raising a good man or woman" might have been. Instead, it's exposing them to Mozart in the womb, golf in preschool, and French in first grade.

Beyond lessons and sessions and other things you can purchase, we've also somehow conflated success in parenting with *doing for* our children. So we make a sandwich or fetch a snack long past the time they can reasonably do so themselves; we take care of household chores or outside maintenance ourselves—or outsource it—rather than teaching our kids to wield a dust cloth or handle a rake, as I discussed in Chapter Seven. And we sit down to play what feels like four hundred straight games of Candy Land, instead of requesting they figure out something to do on their own or with siblings or friends.

We *want* to do a lot of these things, sure. But we also feel, often, that we *have* to do them. Anything less is failure.

The basic rule seems to be this: if there's something we *can* do, or try, or sign up for, or buy that can enrich our children, we *should* do it, try it, sign up for it, or buy it.

Because if you don't (try it, buy it, sign up for it, show up and be enthusiastic about it), you have *failed*. Your child. And that's just unacceptable. The problem with this determination to *not fail* is that it leaves parents spinning their wheels, gasping as they try to keep up. And no one wants to admit that keeping up with the infinite possibilities we have for nurturing and improving, and being with and doing for our children, is, well, impossible. The number of enriching programs or videos you can buy for your baby, or the number of toddler classes you can sign up for, just keeps expanding. Later, the amount of lessons, sports, and other activities you can indulge in *never stops*. What's worse, the pressure never lets up.

> The problem with this determination to *not fail* is that it leaves parents spinning their wheels, gasping as they try to keep up.

But what does going to Mommy and Me, signing up for expensive toddler gym classes, or hauling your school-age child from soccer games to basketball clinic to Irish step dancing to Suzuki violin lessons have to do with *not failing*? Aren't these good things, and don't they represent opportunities that we may not have had ourselves? Isn't one of the main aims of perpetuating another generation to improve it? Give it better than we got? Sure it is. What's different now is the inescapable sense that you *have to* do all you can, even more than you reasonably can. What's different now is the loss in value of just the normal, everyday things that we naturally and effortlessly do as parents to "improve" on what our parents were able and willing to do for us. What's different now is that defining "mommy and me" in the lowercase, or allowing fallow post-school afternoons, are not personal or familial (or even economic) choices but are instead things that feel wrong somehow.

The must-do's are driving parents crazy, although many of us don't necessarily realize why. The notion that getting together with ten other moms and toddlers and gluing construction-paper circles to create snowmen and shaking maracas gives your child an edge is way out of balance. Even more wildly off the mark is the notion that *not* gluing those circles and shaking those maracas labels you a bad mom. It starts before Mommy and Me (which I don't intentionally bash, honestly!), with the idea that you can never leave your child alone to settle his infant gaze on something as simple as you washing a dish, or that you can never let the baby recline in his bouncy seat or on a blanket on the floor while you do crunches or read a magazine. Because that's a great big FAIL.

Failing Your Kids Wasn't My Idea!

Before you start thinking this Mean Mom dreamed up the idea of failing your kids a little bit each day, let me enlighten you about who *did* make that leap. Take a trip back in time, and consider the ideas of late British psychologist D.W. Winnicott. When I first encountered him, I discovered he's the guy who coined the phrase "the good-enough mother," so right away I fell a little bit in love with him. Winnicott also said that not only are minute failures salutary for your child, but they are actually the very *key* to raising psychologically healthy children.

I started my semi-love-affair with the late Dr. Winnicott a couple of years ago, when I was interviewing a child development expert for an article I was writing. It wasn't *about* him, but this expert I was interviewing tossed out the phrase *fail your child, a little bit, every day* to illustrate another point. Right away, a lightbulb started blazing in the back of my brain. I got off the phone, wrote the article in question, and then sat and thought about *failing your child. A little bit. Every day.*

Winnicott's point is not that mothers (or fathers) should neglect feeding, clothing, sheltering, or otherwise nurturing their children. In fact, he was a big proponent, as I'll explain in a minute, of responding more or less seamlessly to a newborn's needs. What he meant is that when we continue to rush to the crying baby when he's no longer technically quite so helpless, we've confused virtue—or success—with fear of failure.

What Winnicott was saying is that it's the small failures—the moments when you don't exactly pull the rug out from under your child, but tug on the rug's fringe just a teeny-tiny bit—that compel our children to grow, to stretch, to learn. It's when you *don't* do something for your child, something he's on the cusp of being able to do, that he makes and strengthens the neural connections necessary to learning to do it himself. And it's not just the doing that he's learning. It's the vastly more important *feeling* that he can do it: the sense of competence, autonomy, and whatever the baby/child equivalent to a puffed-out chest might be. By failing your child on this minute, continual, daily basis, you are, quite literally, helping his brain grow.

Here's how it works. When a baby is born, he needs near total preoccupation from his primary caregiver. Winnicott, in an evocative turn of phrase, said that in the newborn period, there's no separate infant and mother; there's just a nursing couple. (Love that!) But he goes further to say that a good-enough mother intuitively knows when to slowly, gradually provide little time lags between need (crying baby) and response (food, interaction, cuddling). No, no, no, it's *not* leaving a crying baby inconsolably in his crib, or sitting miserably in a dirty diaper. Instead, it's knowing that the baby can *handle* waiting just a second or two (and gradually more), before you pick him up. In that nanosecond, as the baby is confronting and coping with discomfort (remember, for such a brief period of time it's barely a blip at first), he's *learning that he's competent.* A nanosecond at a time. He also knows (the baby, that is, not old D.W.) that his needs *are* going to be met. He knows it because his mom's been there from the start, with her full-to-bursting boobs and her encircling arms and her (to the baby) intoxicating scent.

> By failing your child on this minute, continual, daily basis, you are, quite literally, helping his brain grow.

In those nanoseconds, which increase in tiny increments, he never "forgets" that Mom is there, and certainly he never despairs of getting his needs taken care of; but he learns that there's an awful lot he can do to fill the gap in the meantime.

He learns he's got a brain and boundaries between himself and the adults who spawned him. He learns *who he is*. And remember, though Winnicott devoted a lot of professional time and thought to the mother-and-baby pair with this theory, the way I think about it, it holds up throughout a child's life—and of course for fathers, too.

Okay, so let's rouse ourselves from that dusty old analyst's couch for a minute and think about what these minute failures might mean for our kids as they grow. In fact, what *are* minute failures, now that it's clear we're not talking about leaving your baby in a locked car or never bothering to take him out in the sunshine? Minute failures, the kind that make baby neurons fire merrily away, are the little things we do, or can do, to back off and *let him*. Remember those short-lived and supremely annoying talking car alarms: "You're too close to the vehicle! Step *away* from the vehicle!" That's the idea. Don't hover so much. Let the baby be for a minute and see what happens. Maybe she can find her thumb on her own (and wow, what a skill to have under her baby belt, right?).

Let's say you're taking your six-month-old for a walk in the stroller, and she starts fussing. Maybe, instead of immediately hanging over the stroller (just think how big and imposing your face is, all up in hers) to try to soothe or distract her, you should just keep walking, maybe singing a tune or talking to her calmly, and see. Perhaps she'll figure out that watching the world go by or feeling the breeze on her face as you stroll is just distracting and interesting enough to cure her of her case of the wah-wahs.

Let's say you're picking up your four-year-old from day care or preschool, and he's struggling to put that day's art project into his backpack, hanging on the hook with his name above it. He can't quite figure out that the job would be easier if, say, he took the pack *off* the hook first. Instead of coming over and *taking* over, give it a minute for him to try to work out the problem. (Just don't let it get to total frustration mode.)

Now let's say your six-and-three-quarters-year-old son (mine, for example) is having trouble with his no-training-wheels bicycle. Do you run awkwardly along behind him, holding the back of his seat? Sure you do. But for how long? Letting go allows the possibility for failure, not to mention minor crashes. But it also sets the stage for success, which is entirely his (even though you're the one standing there in the middle of the road unabashedly shouting, "That's *my* baby! Go, baby, go!").

And now, let's say you have a twelve-year-old who comes home from middle school feeling terribly dejected (and from what I understand from parents of middle schoolers, this is more or less the default state of things). You find out that there's a party that weekend that she's not invited to. Is your impulse to hug her and offer cupcakes, or is it to pick up the phone and call the other student's mother to find out why the lack of invite? The cupcakes are a good idea (usually they are, in my opinion). The phone call? Not so much. I'm not saying your daughter would have "failed" by not being invited to the soiree, but there is in a sense a feeling of failure for her in knowing she's left out this time. It's sad, and until it starts to feel better or she finds different friends or there's a different party that she *is* asked to, she has to own that sad/failed feeling.

Finally, let's say your teenage daughter forgot to tell you that dance-class sign-ups ended last Saturday. Do you let her own the error and not take dance, or not the class she wanted? Whose responsibility was it to make sure the deadline didn't pass? Or let's say your son did kind of a slap-dash job on that history paper or English essay. Do you, upon seeing it the night before it's due, help him rewrite it? If so, how much of it?

You're with me, right? If you do all these things for your child—soothing her every fussy moment, packing up every backpack, hanging on to the back of the bicycle for too long, fixing everything from social disappointments to school mishaps, *your child never gets the chance to learn where her competence starts.* You need to let them fail by *failing them.*

It's all so crazily logical, isn't it? And yet like much of parenting, our emotions get the better of us, or maybe it's the peer pressure, but for today's parents, it's neither easy nor natural to keep Winnicott's ideas front of mind. It's hard to fail, harder to do so with pride, and harder still to see past the fear of failure to get a glimpse of the benefits of doing so. And they're big! Here's what *failing your child, a little bit, every day* might yield you:

+ A baby who figures out how to soothe himself back to sleep at night. Because, sure, you can get up multiple times a night to lull and soothe and feed, but at what point, if you keep that up, do you (a) lose your mind from sleep deprivation; and (b) end up with a child, *way* past diapers, who cannot figure out how to settle himself down at night? **Why failure is good:** Being able to fall asleep is not something babies eventually do; it's a learned skill. Guess who has to teach it? You. And guess how you do it? Yeah, you got it.

+ A baby who, even in the throes of separation anxiety, understands that the sitter's okay after all (and Mom always comes back). Because yes, you can avoid hiring a sitter or having your mom come by to watch the kid, virtuously believing that if your baby cries when you hand her over and you snatch her right back, you're doing her a favor (she needs you, right?). But really what you're doing is denying her the opportunity to learn what life looks like from Grandma's arms, or what another caregiver's idea of play is, or the sweet, sweet feeling of connecting with you again after an absence. **Why failure is good:** It helps your child learn that she can receive care from multiple people, and survive quite handily in between bouts of nonstop *you*.

+ A toddler who picks up the skill—not to mention earns the great and lasting joy—of figuring out how to play *near* you, when he can't play *with* you. Swoop down on to the floor when your little one holds up a block or a doll with a "come hither" pout one too many times, and he never figures out the thousand-and-one ways he can play with his toys using his own imagination. He also never learns the kind of patience he needs to wait for you. Not only that, but *you* never get the real-time evidence of the fact that simply saying, "Not right this minute, honey," won't cause lasting psychological damage. "Not right this minute, honey" holds great power, for you and for your child. **Why failure is good:** Your child hones his own creativity and play skills, and you get head-clearing space. Autonomy for both of you: priceless!

+ A preschooler who cheerfully waves good-bye (or, as was the case with my sons, barely registers your absence when you leave) at drop-off time. It's hard for a mom so virtuously invested in the happiness of her child not to view that child's clinging reluctance to separate as a badge of honor. Sure, I'm as guilty as the next mom of wanting my child to *love* me unreservedly. I just don't fancy deriving love from his sobbing attachment to my legs. **Why failure is good:** Isn't this obvious? Your child should be dashing off to school with joy, right?

+ A school-age child who knows that if he writes an "n" that looks like an "h," he's the one who's going to miss a point on the spelling test. Tempting as it may be to point out a simple handwriting error to a teacher to preserve your child's 100-percent-streak on first-grade spelling tests, allowing your child to own his mistake is a better outcome than a whole stack of perfect scores. **Why failure is good:** Neatness does count in life (that means in the actual as well as the metaphorical sense). Being responsible for one's own work should start early.

The Self-Sufficiency Question

You by now see here that I'm pushing self-sufficiency. But I would never suggest that desiring to raise self-sufficient children is mutually exclusive to making those children feel loved.

I had an interesting conversation with my older son when he was about seven. We were in Florida, on our annual pilgrimage to my parents' winter home, and having two restless little boys means we spend a lot of time looking for kid-friendly activities. We ended up, one day, at Lion Country Safari, and my boy and I were talking about some snakes we'd seen. Let me say here that my eldest is a deeply, charmingly (and sometimes alarmingly) sensitive child. I know many children, if not most, have strong emotions and naturally expansive, caring souls. My kid takes that natural bent to the extreme, as you'll see in a bit.

At the time, he was right at the start of that stage where kids begin pressing harder for privacy and autonomy (not to mention more computer time). Also, being a regular kid, he was able and willing to fluidly relate his experience to the animals, or in this case reptiles, he encountered. He asked me about the snakes' parents, and I reminded him that snakes, like all reptiles, don't hang around their babies. "Sweetie, the mother snake lays her eggs, then leaves. When the babies hatch, they're on their own."

Fat tears welled up in my supersensitive boy's eyes, because he couldn't imagine the snake children having to fend for themselves. ("But aren't the babies scared and lonely? Would you have done that to *us*?") That being said, once I consoled him, he brightened up when he considered the positive side of the situation: "If I were a snake, then I could have as much computer time as I wanted!" I gave him a hug, declining to point out that without fingers (or a higher-functioning brain), having more time to create PowerPoint presentations or search YouTube for *SpongeBob SquarePants* videos would be lost on a motherless reptile anyway.

My point is that I'm not looking to be a Reptile Mama, laying my eggs and slithering away so that my children can fend for themselves. But neither do I want my sons to be so helpless, so *spongy*, that real life is daunting in the extreme.

Why *do* so many of today's parents believe that doing everything for their children is the right way to go? Why do we march into principals' offices and demand changed grades, special provisions? Why do we play board games that bore us to tears (I don't mean *ever*, I mean *every time* the kid asks, or *to the exclusion* of anything else we'd rather do or need to do)? I actually can't recall a single time my parents did that; our games were *ours*; the things we did together as a family didn't involve the children's toys. That never felt like abandonment; it felt, actually, quite normal, even preferable. Goodness, if we'd played Life or Sorry with my parents, they might have insisted we play *by the rules*, whereas my sister and I, or our friends, frequently brainstormed new, bent, creative rules to up the fun factor as we played. For example, when we played Life, the one with the little cars filled with pink or blue peg "children," we were either a highly paid doctor or a highly paid lawyer; no way would we take the profession printed on the card you were supposed to draw. We wrote our own futures in that game—and why not? We were playing *by ourselves*.

It's not just about the board games, of course. Why don't we let our children stumble and fall? And why do we forget that letting them stumble and fall also allows them to learn how *not* to stumble the next time?

So, failure. Not a lot, just a little bit, and every day, is the recipe for, wait for it: success.

[10]

Mean Mom Manifesto #10: Prepare Them for the World (Not the World for Them).

So, why *did* you have children?

It's sort of a rhetorical question, because heaven knows I don't have the answer for myself. Or at least, my answer can't be neatly tied up in a bow.

I had children because it's a biological imperative to perpetuate the species; my ovaries tingled, my husband was around and willing (a frequent combination, it must be said), and voilá: baby. I had kids to do my part to keep the population from dipping, which either is or isn't happening, depending on which stats you believe. I did it in an urge not to be forgotten. (Even though if you project far enough into the future, I'm afraid it's inevitable that we all—well, most of us—do ultimately end up forgotten. Have you wandered through any abandoned graveyards lately?) I had children so there might be someone to take care of me when I get old, although having waited a bit to start the process,

I don't plan to get old for a really long time; I have to keep myself healthy until my boys are men, and that's going to be awhile. I did it to expand our broader family, to keep holidays interesting (seriously, seeing the same people year after year gets old; it's nice to inject new faces in the mix, right?), and of course to pass along family traditions, quirks and personality traits, and heirlooms.

I had children to see what they'd look like. Come on, admit this is true for you, too; isn't it neat to see your husband's expressive eyebrows reborn on a fresh face? Or your own hazel eyes and pointy chin in your kid? Or to catch heart-stopping glimpses of the ghosts of your grandparents lurking in your children as they grow? Finally, of course, some of us could answer this as simply as: I had children because I, you know, got pregnant.

But why else do we have children? What I'm getting at here is this: Didn't at least a portion of the reason you had children involve imagining them being all grown up, being *people*, not babies or kids under our semi-control, but actual *citizens of the world*? Someone who might someday discover that there was (is?!) life on Mars. Someone who might write a series of plays to rival Shakespeare or Arthur Miller. Someone who might turn dreaded childhood diseases into historical footnotes. Someone who is at the table when peace is finally brokered between Israel and Palestine, or who writes about it and wins a Pulitzer. Someone who takes the oath of high office and actually has the brains and the guts to do a fantastic job. Someone who brings technology and running water to remote locales, or invents better, smarter, safer ways to feed the world, who educates and informs through actions and words, both spoken and written.

Or maybe you're hoping or dreaming not for accomplishments that warrant fanfare or a place in history, but something simpler, though no less important. Maybe the people you want to raise are folks who can keep a family knit together, who can call their siblings on more than just their birthdays, who can take over cooking the Thanksgiving turkey, who can explain who's who in the old photographs. Someone who will teach their own kids what you taught them. Someone who will stand up, even if they never actually stand out in the wider world. The kind of person of whom neighbors and friends, colleagues and acquaintances will say: "He's a good man," or "She's a good woman."

We can hope for these things, and my guess is we all do. But hope isn't enough. We have to lay some groundwork, while we can, to help turn the babies we create, for whatever reason we created them initially, into good women and men. That's why this final **Mean Mom Manifesto #10** is **Prepare Them for the World (Not the World for Them).**

And it's probably the hardest one.

Thinking Ahead—Way Ahead

Before I had kids, before I'd even met my husband in fact, I had a semi-philosophical discussion with a colleague at the magazine I was then working for. She was a young woman only a year or two out of college, and she'd reached that point at which you wonder: Is this what I studied to do, or to become? Is this all there is for me? She was puzzling out whether being a junior magazine editor was really Doing Something (as opposed to some of the things her friends were up to, such as getting advanced degrees or joining the Peace Corps). I told her that there was, or could be, value in anything you do. I half-jokingly told her that if everyone joined the Peace Corps, there would be no one left for the Peace Corps to *help*.

And then I told her that, as far as I was concerned, if all I did in and for the world was to raise a couple of children who became good citizens of the world someday, that would be enough of a contribution for me.

I remember this conversation so vividly because I meant what I told her quite sincerely, even powerfully, and yet I had not thought about it in those terms at all before that exact moment. It was one of those rare times when something pops out of your mouth and you realize it probably had been wandering unsaid in your brain for years. Then you say it, you hear yourself saying it, and you think: *Yes! That's IT!*

> I am going to take these two little boys I've created and turn them into good men. If it kills me.

Eureka! I have found it! My reason for being in this world. I am going to take these two little boys I've created and turn them into good men. If it kills me.

To even begin thinking about the concept of raising good

women and men, it's necessary to take the long view, which means remembering that babies aren't babies forever, kids aren't always helpless or needy, and teens are halfway out the door already. I admit I have not always been good at this, but I am also beginning to see that the current parenting culture tends to reward and celebrate a shorter view of thinking. We've all heard these terms:

You're in the trenches!

It's baby boot camp!

These are the no-sleep, no-thinking years!

We just have to survive fourth grade/middle school/college applications...

And while, yes, it *is* not only normal but adaptive to absorb yourself into caring for your baby—particularly your first, when you are like a newborn giraffe on skis facing a black-diamond hill in the middle of an ice storm (that is to say, somewhat shaky on how you'll manage to stay upright)—there's an awful lot of emphasis on that stage. Too much, I'd argue. Too much indulgent chatter about *how hard* it is, how you *have to give so much up*, how you *have no time at all* to think about anything, or do anything, that isn't baby related. Or, as they grow bigger, kid-related. Because even after we've graduated from baby boot camp, we keep our heads down and our thoughts almost exclusively short-term, feeling it somehow not just necessary but also virtuous to involve ourselves in the day-to-day happiness of our kids, to the exclusion of thinking about who they'll be someday, in the long term.

Oh, we say we're thinking about the long term; we save for the college careers we picture for our brilliant children; we imagine grandchildren settled at our holiday tables; we carefully save boxes of Matchbox cars or pristine American Girl dolls to give back to our kids at some mythical future moment when we turn to them and they thank us for all we've done for them.

But do we stop to wonder if maybe we've done just a smidge too much? Did our imagining of the future stop there, at dreams on the one hand, and college mutual funds on the other, with not that much thought to the actual, real-life people they'd be, their character? Are we taking the long view?

> We've flipped that balance on its head, spending more time worrying about short-term happiness, what's going on right under our noses at this minute, than we do about the fuzzy, hazy long term.

While parents of my folks' generation and earlier *did* spend more time on the long view than the short one, it seems that we've flipped that balance on its head, spending more time worrying about short-term happiness, what's going on right under our noses at this minute, than we do about the fuzzy, hazy long term.

An Excess of Earnestness

What I find terribly ironic is that it's exactly our earnestness, our well-meaning, almost hyperaware and overeducated approach to parenting, that's most likely to be messing up our kids in the long term, if we take the long view. You think messing up is too strong? Maybe, but maybe not. Go talk to a high-school prin-cipal who gets contacted by parents irate over problems he (or his predecessors) rarely saw crossing their desks before, like why a child didn't get into an honor society when his grade-point average is *only* a half-point shy, or why the teacher can't turn that B into a B plus for the sake of the transcript or the football scholarship.

Go talk to a college dean or admissions officer who fields calls from parents wondering why their child didn't get in, or why, now that she is at school, she's getting poorer-than-expected grades. Go talk to college staff who can't seem to kick parents off campus during freshman week, when the new students are all unpacked and their expensive dorm room accoutrements are all purchased and set up, and there's really no earthly reason they should still be there. Go talk to hiring managers bewildered by new recruits who think it's a straight shot from entry level to the CEO's suite. Go talk to a psychotherapist who treats twenty- and thirty-something young adults who describe perfectly attuned parents who gave them problem-free happy childhoods, and yet who can't quite explain why they feel so rootless, empty, unable to make decisions or commitments.

Yeah, I do think those beating helicopter blades are messing up our kids' ability to just grow up. Do you really think that if baby sparrows had it so good in their nest, that if their mothers were still bringing them juicy worms, without them having to lift a wing feather, they'd still launch themselves into the unknown? You'll notice that the mother bird has to actually *push*.

I've read and heard some interesting arguments for why we're here, in this spot where parents, collectively and as individuals, are focused in so narrowly on their children's here and now; in this spot where everyone gets a trophy just for showing up; in this spot where no failure is termed as such (it's all a "good try!" or a swift mollification with ice cream), presuming any occupation or activity that involves the *possibility* for failure is even allowed.

Is it because we wanted to be cooler than our parents, to blur the lines between kids and adults? Is it because, as I've said before, the world is just more set up for kids' needs and comfort (we've gone all the way to the opposite end of the spectrum from the old "kids should be seen and not heard")? I'm honestly not sure.

I heard an interview just the other day on the radio, with a historian who's come out with a new book about the state of marriage today. She described how one of the issues facing modern marriages is the "royalization" of kids; our kids are the princes and princesses of the house, but we're not kings and queens. We're more like their lowly servants, and at the very bottom of the priority list is our marriages. And, I'd argue, along with a healthy marriage in the low-priority category is any serious estimation of how our little royal highnesses are expected to get along in a world that won't hand them snacks at will—not to mention the TV remote and the car keys.

Our kids are smack at the center of family life. Now, that doesn't sound *awful*, right? Where else should they be—out in the garage? Not at all. But when we stick our kids in the center, we by design shove not just ourselves to the periphery, but also our family *as a whole*. There was a time, let's remember, when it was not at all odd for the kids to do mountains of necessary daily family chores before they even went to school, such as gathering eggs and milking cows. Naturally that doesn't apply anymore to any but a very small subset of American families, but the very notion that kids would be pulling on the same oars as their parents, in pursuit of moving the whole family forward, is a head-scratcher to many of today's parents.

We're raising a nation of individuals, sacrificing our own pursuits, often, for the sake of their happiness, and leaving by the wayside the idea that all family members should sacrifice for the whole, as well as join in the celebration and lift one another up. Instead of a family, we've got multiple demanding fiefdoms.

Sometimes, when I think of the way I see some parents today scrambling around trying to create an ideal world for their kids and around their kids, an image comes to mind of a bride in a ridiculously overwrought dress (think poor doomed Prin-

> When we stick our kids in the center, we by design shove not just ourselves to the periphery, but also our family *as a whole*.

cess Diana at her wedding to Prince Charles back in 1981). Someone—actually a small army of someones—had to hold up that crazy long train of hers, arrange it on the steps of the cathedral so that it draped just so, and presumably had to work out how to pack it into the fairy-tale carriage the new bride and groom rode off in. We're all sometimes like a bunch of overworked bridesmaids, shuttling around in service to our kids (the brides in this metaphor) in giant dresses (the world we're piling onto them).

It's a world our kids are ultimately going to be as unready and unsuited for as poor Diana was; though she made a good show of it for a long time, she was never quite able to hold up under the weight, first of the dress and then of the expectations.

In a similar way (and then I promise I'll drop this metaphor), we try—earnestly and lovingly but wrongheadedly—to hold up and smooth out the world around our kids and before our kids, like the train on that dress or the red carpet the royal bride treads upon, making everything friendly, safe, unchallenging, and unruffled for them.

Childproofing the World

I was thinking again, as I was writing, about my grandmother telling her kids to eat the broccoli on their plates even though they detected bugs in it. Can you imagine that happening today? Of course not—and only in part because most of us buy broccoli that's been so well (or ill) treated with pesticides that there are no bugs. We'd sweep it away and get them something else.

Can you stand another example from the past? You know how, in most youth sports these days, everyone gets a trophy? Losses are glossed over, wins exaggerated. When my father-inlaw was about seven, he wandered over to a group of people playing soccer in a field near his home and asked what was up.

He ended up joining a German-American league *without his parents' knowledge*, at least at first. He played the game until he was an adult and can't recall if his parents ever even *attended* a game, much less cheered his successes or mollified his failures.

I'm not saying my father-in-law's parents were right; they were just doing what parents of that generation did. But they weren't wrong either, in the sense that the result was a man, my father-in-law, who learned very young, in this as well as in other ways, that the world wasn't going to be laid out for him, that he'd have to work his way through it and sometimes feel some pain in the process. His wasn't a "childproofed" existence, certainly, though he was well loved and competently raised (which I know because he, in turn, raised a pretty darned good son!).

Meanwhile, here in the overinvolved present day, our plan has been to childproof the world for them. Instead we should be working to world-proof our children, so that they're able to withstand the slings and arrows of lost soccer games and poor grades and sloppy projects, and skinned knees and friends who do them wrong and teachers who just aren't a good fit. And movies they're not permitted to see and gadgets they have to wait to own, if they are allowed to have them at all.

If you're determined to take the long view, you have to first decide what it is you want to see, ideally, as the end result. Okay, I know what you're thinking: We can do the best we can and prepare for the most amazing outcome, but what if things just sort of…go wrong with our kids? Hey, it happens: You know the old adage about the best-laid plans. You've heard about the black sheep kids, the unexplained failures and disappointments ("but they were such good parents!").

But I'm not talking about *plans*. Plans are things like, "My child will go to Harvard," or "My child will be a professional, like a doctor or lawyer." I'm not even talking about softer, touchy-feely hopes or dreams, such as "My child will be happy" or "My child will feel safe and secure." All of these things are individual, cultural, social—and subject to change. The vague and mushy "My child will be happy" is the most malleable of all: Who says what "happy" means? What if your definition of happy is "good job, comfortable house, nice family, great vacations," and your eventually-adult-child's definition is "surfing a good wave"?

No, to me, the long view is less about imagining either grand plans (Harvard) or mushy ones (sweet, sweet happiness), and more about giving kids the internal wherewithal to define their own hopes and dreams, plans and schemes. To have strength and independence, an internal compass, brainpower, and creativity enough to *make* plans, and guts enough to put plans into action, or to shift direction when the going gets tough, or goes sour completely.

> The long view is less about imagining either grand plans or mushy ones, and more about giving kids the internal wherewithal to define their own hopes and dreams, plans and schemes.

I want my children to feel my own and my husband's love and, in turn, understand what it means to give it. I want them to see us working hard and understand the value of it. I want them to feel gratitude and empathy. I want them to feel their place in the history of their family. I want them to be independent. And that last one? That's the hardest one, because I want it the most of all, and it's the one that by definition means *they will leave me.*

But wasn't that the idea all along?

How to Take the Long View

But before we start weeping sad/happy tears thinking about college graduations and wedding aisles and becoming grandparents, let's talk about how we get to the place—when our kids are still quite young—where we can even think about taking the long view. Taking the long view involves plenty of things, but it starts with basic attitudes and practices in early childhood. It may surprise you to know this (though if you've read this far, you should be starting to understand it!), but letting go, letting your kids *leave you as independent people and citizens of the world* starts pretty much right after you have them. A few long-view steps to take:

Don't sweat the childproofing

Safety is smart, sure. But going overboard with it sets two unwelcome precedents. First, it intensifies your own suspicion or belief that danger lurks around every corner, which means you have the responsibility to erase any and all possibility for danger—a task not unlike Sisyphus shoving that rock up the mountainside over and over. Second, over time—as you over-shadow and overprotect your kids—the children internalize the "I'm so fragile" message. The result? You spend way too much time and mental energy protecting your children, wrapping them in metaphorical bubble wrap, with great potential to suf-focate their growth.

So while I *am* a proponent of decent, provable, and smart safety measures, I also think there's an underlying insidious-ness to quite a lot of the childproofing oeuvre. I believe in the efficacy of car seats and am horrified by the idea that my mother took my newborn sister home in a bassinette-like basket that hung, via curved metal hooks, onto the back of the car's bench seat. One bump and the baby would have flown out—and it was July, so the windows were probably open in the car, given that there was no AC. Bye-bye, baby! And yet, it's all gone too far; we've gone from sensible safety measures to the belief that we can eradicate any hazard, ever.

Someone got hurt on a too-fast playground merry-go-round? Off they go to the scrap heap, replaced by equipment that, while safe, can sometimes limit imaginative play (and we still follow them around on the playground, arms outstretched to catch wayward toddlers before they tumble).

I believe in slats on cribs that are spaced so that a child's head can't get stuck, in bicycle helmets, in laws that require cars to stop when school buses do; these and other innovations and reg-ulations are provable ways kids are safer now than they used to be. But the line that was drawn from these improvements to such products as knee pads for new crawlers (I'm sorry; are *your* baby's knees not naturally padded by, you know, *fat*?) and little mesh bags so your toddler can suck—rather than chew—on pieces of fruit give us the message the world is full of sharp edges *that we have to smooth out,* and that—here's the larger point—our kids are otherwise ill equipped to navigate around on their own.

The problem is only a little bit an issue of how much we unnecessarily spend on this stuff—whole catalogs and stores filled with things our mothers might look at as though they were strolling through a museum of oddities: *What is* this *for?!* The problem is the add-on effect of our devotion to safety products. You get one essential thing, and then there's the *other* thing that goes with that that you *also* have to have, and before you know it, you've got a houseful of only marginally useful stuff, all of which prevents you *and* your child from seeing that child as competent. The perception is that neither you nor your child can be trusted: you to warn your child away from a hot stove; your growing child from understanding that those knobs he can just barely reach are not for him to touch.

Now, I know that all kids are different; you can give birth to one child who never seems to notice that there are cabinets at his eye level, and another who'd be in the cleaning supplies the minute you turn your back. For that child, yes, cabinet locks (or a good sturdy rubber band, come on) are smart for your peace of mind and for fewer emergency-room visits. It's the *automatic assumption* that every gadget is necessary—that every child is about to tumble from a stair landing; that no child can be asked to sit and drink out of a regular cup; that every sharp edge is gunning for your tender child's body—that ends up, eventually, infantilizing the lot of them.

If they've fallen, let them get up—on their own

Too much swooping in to pick up and fix up can be just as much of a damper on kids growing up competent and confident as over-childproofing their surroundings. And by the way, working out how to do it on their own is going to involve some failure (see Chapter Nine). Don't fear failure!

One of my best college friends was raised by a pair of child psychologists. Interesting couple. Anyway, I remember my friend's dad telling a story of watching a baby he knew navigate around the living room. Some couch cushions littered the floor, and a toy this kid wanted sat on the other side of a pillow that was *just* big enough to provide a "can I climb over that?" challenge. My friend's father watched as the child tried again and again, with growing frustration, to launch his little body over the pillow. Others in the room wanted to swoop in and help—to move the pillow, to get the kid the toy, or (duh!) to show the toddler that he could simply go *around* the pillow instead of *over* it. This guy stopped them. "Let him try; he'll figure it out." And he did. And boy, was he pleased with his own small victory. This is a sweet story, and of course the value of letting the kid figure his way around the pillow is instructive: *of course* I'd like to do that, you'd say.

But what if instead of watching your ten-month-old crawling around a carpeted living room, you were instead watching your six-year-old trying to work his way across some monkey bars? Would you try to help? What if he fell? How quickly would you dash over to soothe him? I am not suggesting you turn your back on a first-grader wailing as blood runs down his leg, of course. But remember, my question was how *quickly* you'd sprint to his side. Because it's in that small moment between gripping the last monkey bar and either falling or figuring out how *not* to fall this time that boosts your child's confidence—and his growth toward real, no-kidding, lasts-all-his-life confidence.

Quit apologizing for their behavior

He's tired (that's why he smacked his sister or threw his plate of food on the floor). She's bored (that's why she's acting out at the holiday dinner table). She has no one her age to play with (that's why she has to be entertained whenever you visit a home without kids, even at the expense of your own fun with whoever's hosting you). I believe I've mentioned this immutable fact before, but it bears repeating (as if you didn't know it already): Kids are *smart*. They hear *everything* you say. And they internalize it. If you're giving them a behavioral out again and again, guess what? They buy it, hook, line, and sinker. "I'm just bored! I need stimulation! I need a reward for being good!"

When I was a child, there was *nothing* to do at my grandparents' homes, which we visited often. Nothing, that is, that was the same as what we had available to us at home: There was no rusting metal swing set in the backyard, no closet filled with games and toys. No Barbie camper van and vinyl-sided box filled with her clothes and tiny spike-heeled shoes. I wonder if it ever occurred to my parents—much less to my siblings and me—to *bring our toys with us*, but we didn't. And certainly, my parents never, ever complained to their folks that there was nothing at their homes to entertain us kids, or that their homes or yards weren't "safe" for us to play in. We drove there, we said hello, maybe Grandpa slipped us a dollar bill to squirrel away in our piggy banks when we got home, and then we entertained ourselves. Me personally? I was endlessly captivated by the gold-toned brush and comb set, and the glass perfume bottles, set on the mirrored vanity tray in our grandmother's room, or the soup can on my grandfather's desk, filled with pens he'd collected on his travels. If we were lucky, Grandpa's garage would be open and heaven knows what we'd find there (I'm sure it was all wildly unsafe). But I wonder: had my parents, even once, excused some bit of bad behavior with an apologetic "Oh, she's just bored, we should have brought some toys," would we have felt, on the next visit and thereafter, *entitled* to such accommodation and entertainment?

Let them roam as free as possible

In my school district, kindergarten children are not let off the bus if a parent or designated guardian is not there. Even if the bus driver knows my neighbor (he does), and said neighbor offers on the spot to take my child off the bus until I get back (she would), it's a no-go. I guess I get that—to a point. After kindergarten, it's no problem for a child to get off the bus without falling into the waiting and protective arms of a parent, but dang if it ever actually happens. Last year, I informed my newly minted third-grader that I wouldn't be collecting him at his stop in the afternoon. He'd started a different school than his first-grade brother, with different hours. I did not fancy—especially come winter—getting myself geared up for the short walk up the block four times a day. My son was fine with it. No, scratch that—he was *delighted* to take that walk (well, run in his case) solo. But the first few weeks of school caused no small measure of confusion between the bus driver and curious fellow parents. Eventually everyone calmed down and my child managed the walk down the hill and around the slight curve of the street, and up our driveway to the kitchen door.

Back in the day? My sister and I walked off down the street, around the corner (and out of sight) to the next street for our bus stop, along with a mixed bag of students of all ages, but no parents. It was a mildly lawless place, our bus stop; no real danger (we knew to stick close to the curb), but some serious shenanigans. And when the tall eighth-grader kept stealing my hat and holding it up above my head? I got upset, but I never told my mother. Why? Didn't occur to me. Home was *her* place. The "wilds" of our suburban map of streets, woods, parks, and backyards? Ours. She didn't know that we played King of the Hill at the site of a new home being built on the next street (heavens, think of it: we played *in the freshly dug basement* of a house, and no one knew or cared).

When I fell off my bike, I went home and got a Band-Aid (or a neighbor took me into her house and cleaned my scrapes).

When I sold Girl Scout cookies, I put on my uniform and traveled the neighborhood on my own, with my order form, hoping that, like last year, Mrs. Schlie would ask me in and give me a glass of orange juice while she made her choices. Can you imagine that today? Didn't think so. The freer kids can roam, the less fragile they feel, the more hearty, resourceful, and mature they end up.

Don't make it about you

Because it's not. Plenty of us talk a very good game on this subject. We sign them up for soccer and T-ball and hip-hop dance and ice-skating so *they* can enjoy these things, right? Dig deeper under the claim you might be making that you just want your child to find his passion: Do you really want that, alone, or do you want them to find your passion, to show others that you have a brilliant dancer or goal-scoring striker on your hands? And *are* they really enjoying it all, or are they trooping along for you? It's not just about activities you join and pay for either.

Take me, for example: As a child, the *only* thing I cared to do was read. I read everywhere, at all times, insatiably. Now, if I say that I want my sons to be excellent readers, too, if I want them to know that feeling of never being bored if you have a book—even one you've read three times before—that's not *bad*, is it? Well, no. But also yes. Because it's quite possible that I have been pushing it on them, which is much more about me than it is about them, and I realized that recently, to my shame. My older son is a good reader; he's proficient. He reads fluidly and well. But picking up a book is just not something he does when he has a choice of doing *almost* anything else.

I've gone on and on (and on) to both my boys about my passion for reading as a kid, how I'd take stacks of books from the library, take them home, and sit on my bedroom floor reading until my butt fell asleep or it was dinnertime, whatever came first. How I read in cars, even on the shortest of trips, to the endless frustration of my sister, who'd rather play (reading made her carsick). I thought these stories would make them laugh and intrigue them and compel them to be *just like me* in that regard, so *I* could point at my kids and say, "They're big readers, my boys!" One morning, when I was asking my son to spend a few minutes reading instead of, say, playing the Wii game, his eyes welled up with tears and he said, "I like to read, Mom, I do. I just don't like it *as much as you do*." He ended up feeling intimidated by the very stories I told in hopes of engaging him. My point is that while I was trying to impart a valuable skill, I was instead trying to relive it through him. But if I—or you—try to remake kids in our image, we aren't giving them breathing room to burnish their own image.

Out of the Nest

The thing about kids is this: They are people. Their own people. Now, of course, if you *want* a sparrow that hangs around the nest waiting for the next worm to be dropped into his mouth (the human equivalent is the home-from-college kid who calls you at work wondering what there is to eat, and it's not that there's no food in the fridge or pantry, but that he has no clear idea how to synthesize the bounty into something edible, and can you come home soon and do it for him, please?), then by all means, continue to make sandwiches and tie shoes and make excuses and interfere between kids and teachers and all the rest. But if you don't?

Long view, my friend.

Now listen, I know what some of you may be thinking here: Don't I want, when my boys are grown men (a thought that reliably heaves a lump up into my throat, in case you were wondering), to still have them around, in my life? Not many baby sparrows come back to the nest for whatever the bird equivalent of Thanksgiving is (hint: probably doesn't involve eating turkey).

I do want my kids to come back to my home, want them to feel that it's always their home, too. I want them to rely on me, call me when they're sad or need advice, share the details of their work lives and love lives (within reason!), and—hopefully this is in the cards for all of us—enjoy parenthood themselves with me in the picture.

But before they come back to us as these full-grown adults (Lump! Tears!), they have to leave. And to leave, they need the tools to do so, on their own sturdy feet, with their own fine minds, with their own clear and hopeful hearts. Making them happy isn't our job; that's their job. But the other stuff? Laying the foundation of those sturdy feet and fine minds and clear and hopeful hearts? *That's* our job.

About the Author

Denise Schipani writes about parenting, health and fitness, relationships, and family for a wide variety of print and online publications. A former magazine editor, she can't help but mentally edit restaurant menus and PTA flyers. She blogs at ConfessionsofaMeanMommy.com. A lifelong New Yorker (except for two years in London that turned her into a committed Anglophile), Denise lives on Long Island with her husband and two sons. And no pets, unless you count the spiders that reside in the washing machine. Find out more at DeniseSchipani.com.